# COMPLETING ALL INITIATIVES

## A Guide to Success

**SREEKUMAR V T**

# PREFACE

Welcome to "Completing All Initiatives: A Guide to Success." In a world filled with endless opportunities and ambitious goals, the journey from inception to completion is often the most challenging yet rewarding aspect of any endeavor. This book is crafted as a guide to empower you with the insights, strategies, and mindset needed to navigate this journey successfully.

Embarking on any initiative, whether personal or professional, requires a blend of determination, planning, and adaptability. Throughout these pages, we delve into the intricacies of completing what you start, exploring the psychological aspects of commitment, the importance of setting realistic goals, and the strategies to overcome hurdles that may emerge along the way.

In our fast-paced world, where distractions abound and priorities shift, understanding the power of completion becomes a crucial skill. "Completing All Initiatives" is designed to be your companion, offering practical advice on time management, habit formation, and effective teamwork. It aims to equip you with the tools necessary to stay focused on your goals, celebrate milestones, and navigate the inevitable challenges that accompany any significant undertaking.

This guide is not just a collection of principles but a roadmap based on real-world experiences, incorporating insights from successful individuals who have mastered the art of seeing projects through to completion. As you embark on this journey with us, consider this book a resource, a mentor, and a source of inspiration.

May these pages inspire you to embrace the pursuit of completion, cultivate resilience in the face of setbacks, and celebrate the achievements that come with finishing what you start. Your success story begins here, and "Completing All Initiatives" is here to guide you every step of the way.

Best wishes on your journey to success!

SREEKUMAR V T

# COPYRIGHT WARNING

All rights reserved. No part of this publication may be reproduced, distributed, or transmitted in any form or by any means, including photocopying, recording, or other electronic or mechanical methods, without the prior written permission of the publisher, except in the case of brief quotations embodied in critical reviews and certain other non-commercial uses permitted by copyright law.

Unauthorized reproduction or distribution of this copyrighted work is illegal and may result in civil and criminal penalties. The publisher and author assume no responsibility for the unauthorized use or misuse of the material contained in this book.

For permission requests, please contact the publisher at vtsreekumar123@gmail.com

Copyright © 2023 by SREEKUMAR V T

All rights reserved.

# CONTENTS

1. Setting the Stage: Understanding the Power of Completion
2. The Psychology of Commitment: Overcoming Procrastination
3. Strategic Planning for Success: Breaking Down Your Initiatives
4. Building a Solid Foundation: Setting Realistic Goals
5. Staying Focused: Overcoming Distractions in Your Journey
6. The Power of Consistency: Establishing Productive Habits
7. Navigating Challenges: Overcoming Obstacles Along the Way
8. Effective Time Management: Maximizing Your Productivity
9. Teamwork and Collaboration: Amplifying Your Success
10. Celebrating Milestones: Boosting Motivation Throughout
11. Adapting to Change: Flexibility in the Pursuit of Goals
12. Mindfulness in Action: Enhancing Concentration and Clarity
13. The Art of Saying 'No': Prioritizing Your Initiatives
14. Learning from Setbacks: Turning Failures into Stepping Stones
15. Culminating Success: Reflections on a Journey of Completion

# 1. SETTING THE STAGE

## *Understanding the Power of Completion*

In the grand theater of life, every initiative is a carefully scripted act, each scene contributing to the overall narrative of our personal and professional development. Yet, the art of completion often eludes us, leaving projects unfinished and dreams unrealized. In this chapter, we explore the fundamental concept of "Setting the Stage" — a crucial first act in the grand production of completing all initiatives.

### The Genesis of Initiatives

Initiatives, whether they be launching a business, pursuing an educational goal, or committing to a healthier lifestyle, all have a beginning. This genesis is a moment filled with inspiration, excitement, and the promise of a brighter future. Yet, the true power lies not just in starting but in understanding the full scope of what it takes to finish.

### The Psychological Landscape

To comprehend the essence of completion, we must delve into the intricate landscape of the human psyche. Our minds are naturally inclined to seek novelty and stimulation, often leading to the initiation of numerous projects. However, without a deep understanding of our psychological tendencies, we risk falling prey to the allure of new beginnings without seeing them through.

Psychological factors such as fear of failure, perfectionism, and the allure of the next shiny idea can become stumbling blocks on the path to completion. Recognizing these factors is the first step in overcoming them and forging ahead with unwavering determination.

**The Anatomy of Commitment**

Commitment is the glue that holds the stages of an initiative together. It is not merely a promise to oneself but a binding contract with one's aspirations. We explore the anatomy of commitment, dissecting its components and understanding how it evolves throughout the lifecycle of a project.

From the initial burst of enthusiasm to the steady dedication required for the long haul, commitment is a dynamic force that transforms over time. Learning to nurture and sustain this commitment is paramount in ensuring that the stage is not only set but remains illuminated until the final curtain call.

**The Role of Realistic Goal Setting**

The setting of achievable goals is the scaffolding upon which successful initiatives are built. Unrealistic expectations can lead to frustration and burnout, derailing even the most promising projects. In this section, we discuss the art of goal setting — a delicate balance between ambition and pragmatism.

By breaking down overarching objectives into manageable milestones, individuals can navigate the journey more effectively. Realistic goal setting not only facilitates progress tracking but also instills a sense of accomplishment at each stage, fueling the motivation needed to reach the ultimate destination.

**Overcoming Procrastination: A Perennial Foe**

Procrastination, the silent assassin of productivity, can undermine the most well-intentioned initiatives. Understanding the root causes of procrastination and implementing effective strategies to overcome this perennial foe are crucial aspects of setting the stage for completion.

From time management techniques to cultivating a proactive mindset, we explore practical tools to conquer procrastination and maintain momentum. The battle against procrastination is ongoing, and victory requires a combination of self-awareness and strategic planning.

**The Collaborative Symphony**

In the grand symphony of completing initiatives, collaboration plays a harmonious melody. Whether working on a team project or seeking support from mentors and peers, the power of collective effort cannot be overstated. We delve into the dynamics of teamwork, discussing how collaboration can enhance creativity, provide diverse perspectives, and offer a shared sense of responsibility.

Through case studies and real-world examples, we showcase the transformative impact of collaborative endeavors. The collaborative symphony amplifies individual strengths, creating a resonant tune that reverberates throughout the journey of completion.

**The Celebratory Interludes**

Amidst the challenges and triumphs, it is crucial to pause and acknowledge the milestones achieved. Celebratory interludes serve as motivators, fueling the fire of determination. From small victories to major accomplishments, each celebration reinforces the commitment to the initiative and rejuvenates the spirit for the road ahead.

In this section, we explore the psychology of celebration, emphasizing its role in sustaining momentum and cultivating a positive mindset. Learning to appreciate progress is an art that transforms the journey from a grueling marathon into a series of exhilarating sprints.

**Adapting the Script: Flexibility in Action**

No initiative unfolds exactly as planned. Unforeseen challenges, changes in circumstances, and unexpected opportunities demand a level of flexibility in the script. We discuss the importance of adaptability and provide strategies for navigating the twists and turns that inevitably arise.

Through anecdotes of resilience and adaptability, we illustrate how successful individuals have embraced change as an integral part of the completion process. Adapting the script does not signify weakness but rather a strength that allows for continued progress despite the unpredictable nature of the journey.

## Mindfulness in Action: Enhancing Concentration and Clarity

In the age of constant distractions, cultivating mindfulness is a powerful tool for maintaining focus and clarity. We explore mindfulness techniques that can be seamlessly integrated into daily routines, enhancing concentration and fostering a deep connection with the task at hand.

From meditation practices to practical tips for staying present, we delve into the transformative impact of mindfulness on the completion journey. By incorporating these practices, individuals can navigate the complexities of modern life while staying attuned to the nuances of their initiatives.

## The Art of Saying 'No': Prioritizing Initiatives

While enthusiasm may drive us to take on multiple initiatives simultaneously, the art of saying 'no' is a strategic skill that ensures focus on the most critical endeavors. We discuss the importance of prioritization, providing practical advice on evaluating opportunities, setting boundaries, and aligning actions with overarching goals.

The ability to say 'no' is not a rejection of possibilities but a conscious choice to allocate time and energy to initiatives that truly matter. By mastering this art, individuals can avoid the pitfalls of spreading themselves too thin and enhance their capacity for completion.

## Learning from Setbacks: Turning Failures into Stepping Stones

Setbacks are an inevitable part of any journey, and the completion of initiatives is no exception. In this section, we explore the mindset needed to navigate failures and turn them into valuable stepping stones toward success. Resilience, perseverance, and the ability to extract lessons from setbacks are essential attributes that distinguish those who complete initiatives from those who falter.

Through case studies of individuals who have faced adversity and emerged stronger, we draw inspiration from their stories. Learning from setbacks is not a sign of weakness but a testament to the indomitable human spirit that persists in the face of challenges.

### Culminating Success: Reflections on a Journey of Completion

As the final act approaches, we reflect on the transformative journey of completion. Culminating success is not just about reaching the destination but about the evolution that occurs along the way. We explore the importance of reflection, gratitude, and the cultivation of a growth mindset as individuals stand on the threshold of accomplishment.

In this concluding section, we celebrate the power of completion and its enduring impact on personal and professional fulfillment. The journey does not end with one initiative but becomes a continuous cycle of growth, setting the stage for future endeavors.

### Conclusion

"Setting the Stage: Understanding the Power of Completion" is not merely a chapter in a book but a guide that illuminates the path to success. By comprehending the psychological intricacies, embracing commitment, and implementing practical strategies, individuals can set the stage for completing all initiatives.

The journey of completion is a symphony of determination, collaboration, adaptability, and resilience. As the curtain rises on each new initiative, may the insights shared in this chapter serve as a beacon, guiding individuals through the challenges and triumphs that lie ahead.

In the grand narrative of your life, may the act of completion be a resounding crescendo, echoing the fulfilment that comes from seeing every initiative through to its glorious conclusion.

# 2. THE PSYCHOLOGY OF COMMITMENT

## *Overcoming Procrastination*

In the pursuit of completing all initiatives, understanding the intricate interplay of psychological factors becomes paramount. At the heart of this complex dance lies commitment—a force that propels us forward in the face of challenges, yet is often tested by the pervasive adversary known as procrastination. In this chapter, we unravel the psychological nuances of commitment and explore strategies to overcome the persistent foe of procrastination.

### The Essence of Commitment

Commitment is the bedrock upon which successful initiatives are built. It is the unwavering resolve that sustains us through the peaks and valleys of our journey. Yet, commitment is not a static state; it is a dynamic force that evolves over time. To comprehend its essence, we must delve into the psychological realms that influence our ability to stay dedicated to our goals.

Intrinsic vs. Extrinsic Motivation

The roots of commitment are often entwined with the type of motivation driving our initiatives. Intrinsic motivation, fueled by personal passion and a genuine interest in the task at hand, tends to foster stronger and more enduring commitments. On the other hand, extrinsic motivation, driven by external rewards or pressures, may provide a temporary boost but often lacks the staying power needed for long-term commitment.

Understanding the interplay between these motivational forces is essential for cultivating a commitment that withstands the test of time. We explore how to tap into intrinsic motivation, aligning personal values with overarching goals to create a deep and meaningful commitment.

## The Procrastination Puzzle

As commitment takes center stage, it encounters a formidable adversary—procrastination. The art of delaying tasks, procrastination has a profound impact on our ability to stay committed to initiatives. To unravel the procrastination puzzle, we must delve into the psychology behind this common but often misunderstood behavior.

### The Fear Factor

Procrastination is frequently rooted in fear—fear of failure, fear of success, or even fear of the unknown. By identifying and understanding these fears, individuals can address the underlying psychological barriers that contribute to procrastination. We explore practical techniques for reframing fear, transforming it from a paralyzing force into a catalyst for growth.

### Instant Gratification vs. Long-Term Gain

The human psyche is wired to seek instant gratification, often at the expense of long-term goals. Procrastination, in many cases, is a manifestation of this innate tendency. Through the lens of behavioral psychology, we analyze the conflict between immediate rewards and delayed gratification. Strategies for reprogramming our brains to prioritize long-term gain become crucial in the battle against procrastination.

### The Perfectionism Paradox

Perfectionism, while often viewed as a virtue, can paradoxically fuel procrastination. The fear of not meeting impossibly high standards can lead individuals to delay taking action. We explore the perfectionism paradox, providing insights into embracing imperfection as a stepping stone toward progress. By dismantling the myth of perfection, individuals can free themselves from the shackles of procrastination.

## Strategies for Cultivating Unwavering Commitment

Armed with an understanding of commitment's essence and the procrastination puzzle, we turn our attention to practical strategies for cultivating unwavering commitment to our initiatives.

### Goal Clarity and Visualization

Clarity of goals is the compass that guides commitment. We delve into the importance of clearly defining objectives, breaking them down into actionable steps, and visualizing the desired outcomes. Visualization becomes a powerful tool for aligning the mind with the envisioned success, reinforcing commitment on a subconscious level.

### Establishing Rituals and Routines

Rituals and routines create a structure that supports commitment. By incorporating consistent habits into daily life, individuals can mitigate the impact of decision fatigue and maintain momentum. We explore the science behind habits and offer insights into establishing rituals that bolster commitment.

### Accountability Partnerships

The power of accountability cannot be overstated. Forming partnerships with individuals who share similar goals creates a supportive ecosystem where commitment is reinforced through mutual encouragement and shared responsibility. We delve into the dynamics of accountability partnerships, providing guidance on how to establish effective collaborations.

### Building a Growth Mindset

A growth mindset is the antidote to the rigidity that can undermine commitment. Embracing challenges, learning from setbacks, and viewing effort as a path to mastery are key components of a growth mindset. We explore practical exercises and mindset shifts that foster a growth-oriented perspective, enhancing resilience in the face of obstacles.

## Time Management and Prioritization

Effective time management is a cornerstone of commitment. We delve into strategies for prioritizing tasks, setting realistic deadlines, and avoiding the pitfalls of procrastination-inducing time traps. By mastering the art of time management, individuals can create a conducive environment for sustained commitment.

## Real-World Applications: Case Studies in Commitment

To illuminate the strategies discussed, we turn to real-world case studies of individuals who have successfully navigated the intricate dance of commitment and procrastination. These stories serve as beacons of inspiration, illustrating the transformative power of psychological insights and practical strategies in overcoming obstacles.

## The Intersection of Commitment and Well-Being

As we conclude this exploration into the psychology of commitment, we recognize its profound impact on overall well-being. Commitment is not solely about achieving external goals; it is a journey that shapes our internal landscape. We reflect on the symbiotic relationship between commitment and well-being, emphasizing the holistic benefits that extend beyond the completion of initiatives.

## Conclusion

"The Psychology of Commitment: Overcoming Procrastination" is not a mere chapter in a guidebook; it is a roadmap to unlocking the potential for sustained commitment in the face of procrastination's challenges. By understanding the essence of commitment, unraveling the procrastination puzzle, and implementing practical strategies, individuals can fortify their resolve and set the stage for successfully completing all initiatives.

As the curtain rises on the intricate dance between commitment and procrastination, may the insights shared in this chapter empower individuals to navigate the complexities of their psychological landscape. In the grand narrative of completing all initiatives, may commitment emerge as the resilient protagonist, overcoming procrastination's attempts to steal the spotlight.

# 3. STRATEGIC PLANNING FOR SUCCESS

## *Breaking Down Your Initiatives*

In the labyrinth of aspirations and ambitions, strategic planning serves as the compass that guides us toward the realization of our goals. The journey from initiation to completion is a dynamic process that requires meticulous planning, a roadmap tailored to navigate the twists and turns that invariably accompany any significant initiative. In this chapter, we delve into the art of strategic planning, unraveling the layers that comprise a successful roadmap for breaking down initiatives and achieving ultimate success.

### The Blueprint of Strategic Planning

Before delving into the intricacies of breaking down initiatives, it is essential to understand the overarching framework of strategic planning. Think of strategic planning as the blueprint of a grand architectural design, outlining the foundation, structure, and finishing touches of your initiative.

Defining Your Vision and Mission

At the heart of strategic planning lies the articulation of your vision and mission. Your vision is the vivid picture of what success looks like, while your mission defines the purpose and values that will guide your journey. Clarifying these elements sets the tone for strategic planning, providing a north star that illuminates the path ahead.

Assessing the Current Landscape

Before embarking on any initiative, it is crucial to conduct a comprehensive assessment of the current landscape. This involves understanding internal and external factors that could impact your journey. SWOT analysis—evaluating Strengths, Weaknesses, Opportunities, and Threats—becomes a valuable tool in this stage, offering insights into the terrain you are about to traverse.

Establishing Clear Objectives

Strategic planning demands clarity in objectives. What are you aiming to achieve, and how will success be measured? Clear, specific, and measurable objectives provide the milestones that chart progress and illuminate the way forward. These objectives become the building blocks upon which the initiative will be constructed.

Identifying Key Performance Indicators (KPIs)

To gauge progress effectively, identifying Key Performance Indicators (KPIs) is imperative. KPIs are quantifiable metrics that measure the success of specific objectives. Whether it's revenue growth, customer satisfaction, or project completion time, well-defined KPIs act as navigational markers, indicating whether the initiative is on course or requires adjustments.

## Breaking Down Initiatives: The Art of Decomposition

With the strategic planning framework in place, breaking down initiatives becomes the next crucial step. The art of decomposition involves dissecting overarching goals into manageable components, akin to breaking down a complex puzzle into its individual pieces.

Setting SMART Goals

SMART goals—Specific, Measurable, Achievable, Relevant, and Time-bound—serve as the cornerstone of decomposition. Each goal should be specific in what it aims to accomplish, measurable in its progress, achievable given available resources, relevant to the overall vision, and time-bound to provide a sense of urgency. SMART goals create a roadmap that guides your journey step by step.

### Prioritizing Initiatives

Not all components of an initiative are created equal. Prioritization involves identifying the most critical elements that will drive success. By distinguishing between tasks that are essential and those that can be deferred, individuals can allocate time and resources more efficiently, ensuring that energy is directed toward high-impact activities.

### Sequencing and Timelines

The sequence in which tasks are undertaken is a strategic decision that can significantly impact the flow of an initiative. Establishing timelines for each phase creates a sense of structure and urgency. It prevents the initiative from becoming an amorphous, never-ending endeavor and provides a tangible framework for tracking progress.

### Resource Allocation

Strategic planning requires a judicious allocation of resources—financial, human, and technological. Resource allocation involves determining the personnel, budget, and tools required for each phase of the initiative. By aligning resources with priorities, individuals can optimize efficiency and avoid bottlenecks that may impede progress.

### Risk Mitigation

No initiative is without risk, and strategic planning involves a proactive approach to risk mitigation. Identifying potential risks, assessing their impact, and developing contingency plans are integral components of decomposition. This forward-thinking approach prepares individuals to navigate unexpected challenges and ensures that the initiative remains resilient in the face of adversity.

## The Power of Incremental Progress

Breaking down initiatives not only makes them more manageable but also taps into the psychological power of incremental progress. Humans are wired to find satisfaction and motivation in small victories. Each completed task or achieved milestone provides a psychological boost, reinforcing the commitment to the larger goal.

## The Domino Effect of Success

Initiatives, like a series of dominos, gain momentum with each small success. The completion of one task sets the stage for the next, creating a domino effect that propels the initiative forward. Understanding and leveraging this psychological phenomenon is a key aspect of strategic planning for success.

## Building Confidence Through Achievements

Incremental progress builds confidence. As individuals witness the tangible results of their efforts, a sense of self-efficacy emerges. This self-assurance becomes a powerful force, motivating individuals to tackle more significant challenges and persist in the face of obstacles.

## **Realizing Synergies: The Interconnectedness of Components**

Strategic planning goes beyond breaking down initiatives into discrete tasks; it involves recognizing the interconnectedness of these components. Each task is a piece of a larger puzzle, and their synergy determines the overall success of the initiative.

## Cross-Functional Collaboration

Initiatives often require collaboration across different functions or departments. Recognizing the interdependence of tasks and fostering collaboration between diverse skill sets create a more robust and adaptable initiative. Cross-functional collaboration ensures that each component contributes harmoniously to the overarching goal.

## Iterative Feedback Loops

Strategic planning is not a static process; it thrives on feedback and adaptation. Implementing iterative feedback loops allows for continuous improvement. Regular evaluations, stakeholder feedback, and data analysis provide valuable insights that can be used to refine and enhance the strategic plan as the initiative unfolds.

## Flexibility in Execution

While strategic planning provides a roadmap, it's essential to maintain flexibility in execution. Unforeseen challenges or opportunities may necessitate adjustments to the plan. A rigid approach can stifle innovation and hinder adaptability. Embracing flexibility ensures that the initiative remains responsive to changing circumstances.

## Case Studies: Strategic Planning in Action

To illustrate the principles of strategic planning, we turn to case studies that showcase how individuals and organizations have successfully employed decomposition to achieve their goals. These real-world examples provide insights into the practical application of strategic planning principles and offer valuable lessons for those embarking on their own initiatives.

## Overcoming Common Pitfalls in Strategic Planning

Despite its benefits, strategic planning is not immune to pitfalls. Understanding and proactively addressing common challenges ensure a more seamless execution of the plan.

### Overestimating Resources

One common pitfall is overestimating the resources available for the initiative. Unrealistic expectations can lead to frustration and burnout. Strategic planning involves a realistic assessment of available resources and, if necessary, creative solutions for maximizing their impact.

### Underestimating Risks

Failure to adequately assess and plan for risks is another pitfall. Every initiative carries inherent uncertainties, and strategic planning requires a proactive approach to risk management. Acknowledging potential pitfalls and having contingency plans in place mitigates the impact of unforeseen challenges.

### Lack of Communication

Effective communication is the lifeblood of strategic planning. A lack of clear communication can lead to misunderstandings, misaligned priorities, and breakdowns in collaboration. Regular and transparent communication ensures that all stakeholders are informed and engaged throughout the initiative.

Failure to Adapt

Strategic planning is not a rigid set of rules but a dynamic framework that should adapt to changing circumstances. Failure to recognize the need for adaptation can result in a plan that quickly becomes obsolete. Regular evaluations and a willingness to adjust the plan are essential for success.

## The Continuous Cycle of Improvement

As the initiative progresses, strategic planning becomes a continuous cycle of improvement. Evaluating performance, learning from experiences, and incorporating insights into future planning create a self-renewing process that enhances the effectiveness of each subsequent initiative.

## Conclusion

"Strategic Planning for Success: Breaking Down Your Initiatives" is more than a chapter in a guidebook; it is a comprehensive exploration of the foundational principles that underpin successful endeavors. By understanding the blueprint of strategic planning, mastering the art of decomposition, and recognizing the interconnectedness of components, individuals can navigate the complexities of their initiatives with purpose and precision.

As we unravel the layers of strategic planning, may the insights shared in this chapter serve as a guide for breaking down initiatives into manageable, achievable tasks. In the grand narrative of completing all initiatives, strategic planning emerges as the masterful orchestrator, conducting the symphony of success with finesse and strategic precision.

# 4. BUILDING A SOLID FOUNDATION

## *Setting Realistic Goals*

In the grand tapestry of achieving success, the thread that weaves through every endeavor is the art of setting realistic goals. A solid foundation is the bedrock upon which towering achievements stand. As we delve into this chapter, we embark on a journey into the essence of building a solid foundation by setting goals that are not only ambitious but grounded in reality. Welcome to the exploration of "Building a Solid Foundation: Setting Realistic Goals," an integral part of the guidebook, "Completing All Initiatives: A Guide to Success."

### The Power of Realistic Goal Setting

Goals are the milestones that mark our progress, guiding us through the labyrinth of aspirations. While ambition is a powerful driver, the effectiveness of goal setting lies in its realism. Realistic goals serve as a compass, ensuring that our aspirations are not only lofty dreams but tangible objectives that can be achieved through dedication, effort, and strategic planning.

The Pitfalls of Unrealistic Expectations

Before we delve into the art of setting realistic goals, it's crucial to understand the pitfalls of unrealistic expectations. Setting goals that are too ambitious without a foundation in reality can lead to frustration, burnout, and a sense of failure. Unrealistic expectations may create an illusion of progress, but they often crumble under the weight of unattainable demands.

The Psychological Impact of Realism

Realistic goal setting is not about limiting aspirations; it's about aligning them with the current circumstances and available resources. The psychological impact of setting realistic goals is profound. Achieving incremental success builds confidence, motivation, and a positive mindset. Realism fosters a sense of control, empowering individuals to navigate challenges with resilience and determination.

## The Framework of Realistic Goal Setting

Setting realistic goals involves a thoughtful and strategic approach. It requires a framework that considers various factors, from personal capabilities to external constraints. Let's explore the components of this framework:

Self-Assessment and Capability Analysis

Understanding one's own capabilities is the cornerstone of realistic goal setting. This involves a candid self-assessment of skills, knowledge, and experience. Acknowledging strengths and recognizing areas for growth allows individuals to set goals that are challenging yet attainable. Capability analysis provides a realistic baseline for goal setting.

External Environment and Constraints

The external environment, including economic conditions, industry trends, and societal factors, can influence the feasibility of goals. Realistic goal setting involves an assessment of these external constraints. While some factors may be beyond individual control, awareness of external influences enables strategic planning and adaptability.

SMART Criteria: The Guiding Principles

The SMART criteria—Specific, Measurable, Achievable, Relevant, and Time-bound—serve as guiding principles for realistic goal setting. Each goal should be:

- **Specific:** Clearly defined and unambiguous.

- **Measurable:** Quantifiable so that progress can be tracked.
- **Achievable:** Realistic and attainable with the available resources.
- **Relevant:** Aligned with overarching objectives and the current context.
- **Time-bound:** Set within a defined timeframe to create a sense of urgency.

The SMART criteria ensure that goals are not vague aspirations but concrete targets that propel individuals toward success.

Breakdown into Milestones

Realistic goals are often complex, involving multiple steps and phases. Breaking down overarching goals into smaller, manageable milestones provides a roadmap for progress. Each milestone becomes a stepping stone, marking incremental achievements and reinforcing the commitment to the larger goal.

Flexibility and Adaptability

The journey toward any goal is dynamic, marked by unforeseen challenges and opportunities. Realistic goal setting incorporates flexibility and adaptability. Individuals must be open to adjusting their goals based on changing circumstances, feedback, and new information. Flexibility ensures that goals remain relevant and achievable in the face of the unexpected.

## The Psychology of Realistic Goal Achievement

Realistic goal setting goes beyond a mere checklist of tasks; it taps into the psychology of achievement. Understanding the psychological principles that underpin goal attainment enhances the effectiveness of the process:

Intrinsic Motivation

Realistic goals resonate with intrinsic motivation—the internal drive fueled by personal values, passion, and a genuine interest in the task at hand. Intrinsic motivation sustains commitment, providing the emotional fuel needed to overcome challenges. Realistic goals that align with personal values tap into this powerful source of motivation.

Progress Principle

The progress principle, as identified by psychologists Teresa Amabile and Steven J. Kramer, emphasizes the importance of making progress in meaningful work. Small wins and tangible achievements, even in the pursuit of modest goals, create a positive feedback loop. Realistic goal setting leverages the progress principle, ensuring that individuals experience a sense of accomplishment at each stage.

Goal Commitment and Consistency

Commitment to goals is closely tied to their perceived attainability. Realistic goals foster a higher level of commitment, as individuals believe in their ability to succeed. Consistency in goal pursuit is strengthened by setting objectives that are within reach. The commitment-consistency principle, elucidated by psychologist Robert Cialdini, emphasizes the psychological drive to maintain consistency in one's actions.

## Strategies for Effective Realistic Goal Setting

Setting realistic goals is an art that can be honed with strategic planning and intentional practices. Here are strategies to enhance the effectiveness of realistic goal setting:

Prioritize Goals Based on Impact

Not all goals are created equal. Prioritizing goals based on their potential impact allows individuals to focus on initiatives that align with overarching objectives and contribute significantly to success. By distinguishing between high-impact and low-priority goals, individuals can allocate resources strategically.

Leverage the 80/20 Principle

The Pareto Principle, often known as the 80/20 rule, suggests that roughly 80% of effects come from 20% of causes. Applying this principle to goal setting involves identifying the critical few objectives that yield the most significant results. By concentrating efforts on the most impactful goals, individuals maximize their effectiveness and streamline the path to success.

Regularly Review and Adjust Goals

Realistic goal setting is an iterative process. Regular reviews allow individuals to assess progress, identify areas for improvement, and adjust goals as needed. Continuous evaluation ensures that goals remain relevant in a dynamic environment and provides an opportunity for learning and refinement.

Seek Feedback and External Perspectives

External perspectives, whether from mentors, peers, or stakeholders, offer valuable insights into goal feasibility. Seeking feedback provides a holistic view of goals and helps individuals identify blind spots. External perspectives contribute to a more comprehensive understanding of the realistic challenges and opportunities associated with each goal.

Celebrate Small Wins

The celebration of small wins is a powerful motivator. Acknowledging and celebrating incremental achievements reinforces the commitment to realistic goals. This positive reinforcement creates a sense of momentum and contributes to a positive psychological outlook, fostering resilience in the face of challenges.

## Case Studies: Realistic Goal Setting in Action

To illuminate the strategies and principles discussed, we turn to case studies that exemplify the effective application of realistic goal setting. These real-world examples showcase how individuals and organizations have navigated challenges, adapted to changing circumstances, and achieved success through a strategic and realistic approach to goal setting.

## Overcoming Challenges in Realistic Goal Setting

While the benefits of realistic goal setting are evident, challenges may arise. Understanding common hurdles and strategies to overcome them is essential for ensuring success:

Fear of Mediocrity

One common challenge in realistic goal setting is the fear of mediocrity. Individuals may associate realistic goals with settling for less or being content with average achievements. Overcoming this fear involves reframing the perspective on realism, emphasizing that achievable goals set the stage for sustainable success and long-term fulfillment.

External Pressure and Expectations

External pressure, whether from societal expectations or the perceived standards of others, can influence goal setting. Overcoming external pressure involves prioritizing personal values and aspirations. Realistic goals should align with individual motivations and not be dictated solely by external expectations.

Comparison with Others

The habit of comparing one's progress with that of others can undermine realistic goal setting. Each individual's journey is unique, and success is subjective. Overcoming the comparison trap involves focusing on personal growth, celebrating individual achievements, and recognizing that realistic goals pave the way for sustainable success.

Overemphasis on Immediate Results

In a culture that often prioritizes immediate results, the pursuit of realistic goals may be perceived as slow or lacking in impact. Overcoming the emphasis on immediate results involves cultivating patience and understanding that sustainable success is built on a foundation of realistic, incremental progress.

**The Lifelong Journey of Realistic Goal Setting**

As we conclude our exploration into "Building a Solid Foundation: Setting Realistic Goals," it's crucial to recognize that realistic goal setting is not a one-time event but a lifelong journey. It's a dynamic process that adapts to changing circumstances, evolves with personal growth, and serves as a compass throughout various stages of life.

## Continuous Learning and Adaptation

The journey of realistic goal setting is a continuous cycle of learning and adaptation. Each goal achieved, whether small or significant, contributes to personal and professional growth. The lessons learned along the way inform future goals, creating a trajectory of continuous improvement.

## Goal Setting Across Domains

Realistic goal setting transcends professional aspirations; it extends to personal development, relationships, health, and well-being. The principles explored in this chapter are applicable across diverse domains of life, fostering holistic growth and fulfillment.

## Mentorship and Passing on Wisdom

As individuals navigate their journey of realistic goal setting, the role of mentorship becomes invaluable. Passing on the wisdom gained through experience, sharing insights, and guiding others in their goal-setting endeavors contribute to the collective growth of communities and societies.

## **Conclusion**

"Building a Solid Foundation: Setting Realistic Goals" is not merely a chapter in a guidebook; it is a profound exploration into the principles that underpin meaningful achievements. By understanding the power of realistic goal setting, leveraging strategic frameworks, and applying intentional practices, individuals can lay a foundation for success that is enduring and fulfilling.

As we navigate the realms of ambition and reality, may the insights shared in this chapter serve as a compass, guiding individuals toward the realization of their aspirations. In the grand narrative of completing all initiatives, setting realistic goals emerges as the beacon that illuminates the path to success—a path characterized by resilience, fulfillment, and the transformative power of achievable dreams.

# 5. STAYING FOCUSED

## *Overcoming Distractions in Your Journey*

In the cacophony of modern life, staying focused has become a formidable challenge. Distractions lurk around every corner, beckoning us to deviate from our path and divert our attention. Yet, in the pursuit of completing all initiatives, maintaining unwavering focus is not just a desirable skill; it's a prerequisite for success. In this chapter, we embark on a profound exploration of "Staying Focused: Overcoming Distractions in Your Journey," an indispensable guide within the comprehensive book, "Completing All Initiatives: A Guide to Success."

**The Distraction Dilemma**

Distractions are omnipresent in our technologically saturated and information-driven world. From the incessant pings of notifications to the allure of social media and the constant bombardment of information, the distraction dilemma has become a pervasive challenge. Understanding the nature of distractions is the first step in cultivating the focus required to complete initiatives successfully.

The Multifaceted Nature of Distractions

Distractions manifest in various forms—both internal and external. Internal distractions arise from within, such as wandering thoughts, self-doubt, or lack of motivation. External distractions, on the other hand, emanate from the environment, encompassing everything from noisy surroundings to the seductive pull of smartphones.

The Cognitive Cost of Distractions

Distractions exact a cognitive cost that extends beyond the immediate moment of diversion. The brain must continually switch between tasks, leading to cognitive fatigue and a decline in overall productivity. Recognizing the cognitive cost highlights the importance of minimizing distractions for sustained focus.

**Understanding the Psychology of Focus**

To combat distractions effectively, it's crucial to delve into the psychology of focus. Understanding how the brain functions and the factors that contribute to sustained attention provides a foundation for developing strategies to stay focused.

The Role of Neurotransmitters

Neurotransmitters, the chemical messengers in the brain, play a pivotal role in regulating focus and attention. Dopamine, in particular, is associated with motivation and reward. Understanding how neurotransmitters function in the context of focus sheds light on the neurological processes that underpin our ability to stay on task.

The Myth of Multitasking

Contrary to popular belief, the brain is not wired for multitasking. Attempting to juggle multiple tasks simultaneously leads to a phenomenon known as task-switching cost, where cognitive resources are expended in shifting attention. Embracing single-tasking and focusing on one task at a time proves to be a more effective approach for maintaining concentration.

The Power of Mindfulness

Mindfulness, rooted in ancient contemplative practices, has gained prominence as a powerful tool for enhancing focus. By cultivating awareness of the present moment, individuals can mitigate the impact of distractions and sharpen their cognitive abilities. The practice of mindfulness becomes a cornerstone in the journey to stay focused.

**Strategies for Staying Focused**

Armed with an understanding of distractions and the psychology of focus, we turn our attention to practical strategies for staying focused in the midst of a distracting world. These strategies encompass a holistic approach that addresses both internal and external factors.

## Create a Distraction-Free Environment

External distractions can often be controlled by creating a conducive environment. This involves minimizing visual and auditory distractions, organizing the workspace, and setting boundaries to limit interruptions. An environment designed for focus becomes the canvas on which productivity can flourish.

## Prioritize and Set Clear Goals

Clarity in goals is a powerful antidote to distractions. Prioritizing tasks and setting clear, achievable goals provide a roadmap for focus. The sense of purpose derived from well-defined objectives serves as a guiding light, steering individuals away from the detours of distractions.

## Embrace the Pomodoro Technique

The Pomodoro Technique, a time-management method developed by Francesco Cirillo, involves breaking work into intervals, traditionally 25 minutes in length, separated by short breaks. This structured approach leverages the power of focused bursts, preventing burnout and enhancing concentration. Embracing the Pomodoro Technique trains the mind to work with heightened focus during dedicated intervals.

## Leverage Technology Mindfully

While technology can be a source of distractions, it can also serve as a valuable ally in maintaining focus. Utilizing productivity tools, time management apps, and website blockers allows individuals to leverage technology mindfully. By consciously selecting and configuring digital tools, individuals can turn technology from a distractor into an enabler of focus.

## Practice Digital Detox

The constant barrage of digital information can overwhelm the cognitive faculties and contribute to distraction. Implementing periodic digital detox sessions, where individuals disconnect from screens and immerse themselves in offline activities, rejuvenates the mind and fosters resilience against the allure of digital distractions.

Cultivate a Growth Mindset

A growth mindset, as articulated by psychologist Carol S. Dweck, is the belief that abilities and intelligence can be developed through dedication and hard work. Cultivating a growth mindset fosters resilience in the face of challenges, enhances motivation, and contributes to sustained focus. The belief that skills can be honed over time encourages individuals to persevere in the pursuit of their initiatives.

**Navigating Internal Distractions: Mind Management**

Internal distractions, often stemming from the mind itself, require a nuanced approach to mind management. Strategies that address the internal landscape of thoughts, emotions, and motivations play a pivotal role in staying focused.

Mindfulness Meditation

Mindfulness meditation, with its roots in ancient contemplative traditions, has garnered scientific validation for its effectiveness in enhancing focus and reducing distractions. Regular mindfulness practice cultivates awareness, sharpens attention, and provides individuals with the tools to navigate the internal terrain of distractions.

Set Clear Boundaries

Establishing clear boundaries is an effective strategy for managing internal distractions. This involves defining specific times for focused work, delineating between work and leisure, and setting boundaries on activities that may contribute to mental clutter. Clear boundaries create a structured framework that supports sustained focus.

Address Procrastination Head-On

Procrastination is a common manifestation of internal distractions. Addressing procrastination involves understanding its psychological roots, breaking tasks into smaller, more manageable steps, and incorporating accountability measures. By tackling procrastination head-on, individuals dismantle a significant barrier to focus.

Practice Visualization Techniques

Visualization techniques involve mentally picturing the successful completion of tasks or the attainment of goals. Visualization creates a mental blueprint that enhances focus and motivation. Incorporating visualization into daily routines reinforces the connection between actions and desired outcomes, fostering a sense of purpose.

**The Impact of Focus on Initiative Completion**

As we navigate the strategies for staying focused, it's essential to underscore the profound impact that sustained focus has on the completion of initiatives. Focus is not merely a tool for productivity; it is the linchpin that transforms aspirations into tangible achievements.

Quality over Quantity

Sustained focus elevates the quality of work. When attention is undivided, individuals can delve deeply into tasks, exhibit creativity, and produce high-quality outputs. The pursuit of quality over quantity becomes a hallmark of initiatives guided by unwavering focus.

Time Efficiency and Productivity

Focus is a catalyst for time efficiency. By minimizing distractions and embracing single-tasking, individuals optimize their use of time. The result is heightened productivity, as tasks are completed with greater efficiency and accuracy.

Resilience in the Face of Challenges

Initiatives are rarely devoid of challenges. The ability to stay focused in the face of adversity becomes a testament to resilience. Individuals with a mastery of focus navigate challenges with determination, adapting to unforeseen circumstances without succumbing to distraction-induced setbacks.

Sustainable Momentum

Focus creates a sense of momentum that propels initiatives forward. The consistent application of focused effort generates a sustainable rhythm, preventing the initiative from languishing in the doldrums of distraction. Sustainable momentum becomes the driving force behind the completion of initiatives.

## Real-World Applications: Case Studies in Focus

To illuminate the strategies and principles discussed, we turn to real-world case studies that exemplify the effective application of focus in diverse contexts. These case studies provide insights into how individuals and organizations have harnessed the power of focus to overcome challenges and achieve success.

## The Evolution of Focus: Navigating a Digital Age

In the digital age, where information is abundant and distractions are ubiquitous, the evolution of focus becomes a crucial consideration. Strategies for staying focused must adapt to the changing landscape of technology, work environments, and societal expectations.

Technological Mindfulness

Technological mindfulness involves a conscious and intentional approach to digital interactions. Individuals must navigate the digital landscape with awareness, selecting tools that enhance focus, configuring devices for minimal distraction, and cultivating a mindful relationship with technology.

Remote Work and Focus

The rise of remote work introduces a new set of challenges and opportunities for focus. Managing distractions in a remote work environment requires a blend of autonomy, discipline, and effective communication. Strategies for staying focused in remote work settings become integral to the success of initiatives.

## Cultivating Focus in Educational Settings

The ability to stay focused is a critical skill in educational settings. Whether in traditional classrooms or virtual learning environments, students face distractions that can impede academic progress. Cultivating focus in educational settings involves a collaborative effort among students, educators, and parents to create an environment conducive to learning.

## Overcoming Common Challenges in Staying Focused

While the strategies for staying focused are powerful, individuals may encounter common challenges that require specific attention. Identifying and addressing these challenges ensures a more robust and sustainable focus.

### Information Overload

The deluge of information in the digital age can overwhelm cognitive capacities and contribute to distraction. Overcoming information overload involves cultivating information literacy, discerning between essential and non-essential information, and implementing strategies such as content curation.

### Burnout and Mental Fatigue

Prolonged periods of focused work can lead to burnout and mental fatigue. Addressing burnout involves incorporating regular breaks, practicing self-care, and recognizing the signs of mental fatigue. A balanced approach to focus prioritizes both productivity and well-being.

### External Pressures and Time Constraints

External pressures, such as tight deadlines or competing demands, can challenge the ability to stay focused. Overcoming external pressures involves effective time management, setting realistic expectations, and communicating boundaries to manage workload effectively.

### Resistance to Change

Individuals may encounter resistance to adopting new focus strategies, particularly if they have ingrained habits that contribute to distractions. Overcoming resistance to change involves fostering a growth mindset, highlighting the benefits of focus, and providing support and resources for the transition.

## The Holistic Impact: Focus and Well-Being

As we conclude our exploration into "Staying Focused: Overcoming Distractions in Your Journey," it's crucial to recognize the holistic impact that focus has on well-being. Beyond its role in productivity and initiative completion, focus contributes to a sense of purpose, fulfillment, and overall life satisfaction.

### Mind-Body Connection

Focus is intricately connected to the mind-body relationship. Cultivating focus involves not only sharpening cognitive faculties but also fostering physical well-being. Practices such as regular exercise, adequate sleep, and mindfulness meditation contribute to a holistic approach to focus and well-being.

### Flow State and Peak Performance

The state of flow, described by psychologist Mihaly Csikszentmihalyi, is characterized by deep focus, heightened engagement, and a sense of timelessness. Achieving a flow state represents the pinnacle of focus and is associated with peak performance. Understanding the conditions that facilitate flow becomes a key consideration in enhancing focus and overall well-being.

### Work-Life Integration

Staying focused extends beyond professional initiatives; it encompasses the integration of work and personal life. Achieving a harmonious work-life balance involves setting boundaries, prioritizing well-being, and recognizing that sustained focus contributes to both professional success and personal fulfilment.

## Conclusion

"Staying Focused: Overcoming Distractions in Your Journey" is not just a chapter in a guidebook; it is a profound exploration into the art and science of maintaining unwavering attention in a world filled with distractions. By understanding the nature of distractions, delving into the psychology of focus, and implementing practical strategies, individuals can navigate their journey of completing all initiatives with purpose and precision.

As we navigate the complexities of focus, may the insights shared in this chapter serve as a compass, guiding individuals toward the realization of their aspirations. In the grand narrative of completing all initiatives, staying focused emerges as the steady hand that steers the ship through the turbulent waters of distraction, towards the shores of success and fulfilment.

# 6. THE POWER OF CONSISTENCY

## *Establishing Productive Habits*

In the pursuit of success, the adage "consistency is key" reverberates as a timeless truth. The power of consistency lies not merely in sporadic bursts of effort but in the establishment of productive habits that shape our daily actions. As we delve into this chapter, we embark on a profound exploration of "The Power of Consistency: Establishing Productive Habits," an indispensable guide within the comprehensive book, "Completing All Initiatives: A Guide to Success."

**The Essence of Consistency**

Consistency is the steady heartbeat that sustains progress. It is the unwavering commitment to a set of principles, actions, and routines that propel individuals toward their goals. Understanding the essence of consistency involves recognizing its transformative power in shaping habits and influencing the trajectory of initiatives.

The Behavioral Impact of Consistency

Consistency has a profound impact on behavior. When actions become habitual through consistent repetition, they are ingrained in the neural pathways of the brain. This habitualization leads to a seamless integration of productive behaviors into daily routines, fostering a culture of sustained effort.

The Cumulative Effect of Small Actions

Consistency operates on the principle of small actions accumulating over time. Like droplets of water that carve canyons through rock, consistent efforts, even in seemingly modest increments, accumulate into substantial progress. The cumulative effect of small actions is the driving force behind the transformative power of consistency.

**Building Productive Habits: The Consistency Blueprint**

The bedrock of consistency is the establishment of productive habits. Habits are the autopilot of behavior, guiding actions with minimal conscious effort. To harness the power of consistency, individuals must embark on a deliberate journey of habit formation.

The Habit Loop: Cue, Routine, Reward

Understanding the habit loop, as articulated by Charles Duhigg, provides insights into the mechanics of habit formation. A habit comprises three elements: a cue (trigger), a routine (behavior), and a reward. By identifying and intentionally manipulating these components, individuals can shape and solidify productive habits.

Keystone Habits: Catalysts for Change

Some habits, known as keystone habits, have a cascading effect on other areas of life. Identifying and prioritizing keystone habits leverages their transformative power to influence a broader spectrum of behaviors. Keystone habits act as catalysts for change, creating a domino effect that extends beyond individual actions.

The Role of Consistent Environment

Consistency thrives in a stable environment. Establishing a consistent physical and social environment reinforces habits by reducing decision fatigue and creating a context conducive to routine. A consistent environment becomes the canvas on which productive habits are painted.

**Strategies for Habit Formation**

Habit formation is an intentional process that requires strategic planning and conscious effort. Implementing effective strategies enhances the likelihood of habit adoption and long-term consistency.

Start Small with Micro-Habits

The concept of micro-habits involves starting with tiny, manageable actions that serve as gateways to larger habits. By breaking down habits into bite-sized components, individuals mitigate the resistance often associated with change. Micro-habits pave the way for gradual and sustainable habit formation.

Anchor Habits to Existing Routines

Anchoring new habits to existing routines capitalizes on established patterns of behavior. By associating a new habit with a familiar activity, individuals leverage the momentum of existing routines to propel the adoption of new behaviors. Anchoring habits streamlines the integration of consistency into daily life.

Employ Trigger-Based Reminders

Consistency thrives on reminders that prompt action. Leveraging trigger-based reminders, whether through digital tools, physical cues, or time-based alerts, reinforces the habit loop. Consistent, well-timed reminders serve as nudges that keep habits at the forefront of consciousness.

Foster Accountability through Tracking

Tracking progress is a powerful accountability tool in habit formation. Whether through journaling, habit-tracking apps, or peer accountability, the act of recording and reviewing one's consistency creates a feedback loop that reinforces commitment. Accountability transforms consistency from an individual endeavor into a shared commitment.

**The Psychology of Consistency**

The psychology of consistency delves into the cognitive and emotional dimensions that underpin the power of habitual behavior. Understanding the psychological principles at play enhances the effectiveness of efforts to establish and maintain productive habits.

Cognitive Bias and Routine Comfort

Humans exhibit a cognitive bias toward routine and familiarity. The brain seeks comfort in the familiar, and consistent behaviors become ingrained in neural pathways. Recognizing the cognitive bias toward routine allows individuals to leverage the brain's preference for familiarity in building and sustaining habits.

Emotional Rewards and Positive Reinforcement

Consistent habits are reinforced by the emotional rewards associated with their completion. Positive reinforcement, in the form of a sense of accomplishment or intrinsic satisfaction, strengthens the neural connections associated with the habit loop. Cultivating awareness of these emotional rewards enhances the motivational aspect of consistency.

Overcoming Resistance with Consistency

Resistance to change is a natural human tendency. Consistency serves as a counterforce to resistance by gradually acclimating individuals to new behaviors. The incremental nature of consistent efforts minimizes the psychological barriers associated with change, allowing individuals to overcome resistance more effectively.

**Productivity and Consistency: A Symbiotic Relationship**

The relationship between productivity and consistency is symbiotic. Consistency is the engine that drives sustained productivity, and productivity, in turn, reinforces the habit of consistency. Examining the interplay between these two elements illuminates the dynamic synergy that underlies successful initiatives.

Productivity as a Byproduct of Consistency

Consistency creates the conditions for productivity to flourish. When actions become ingrained habits, the mental energy required for decision-making diminishes. This reduction in decision fatigue frees up cognitive resources for focused, productive work. Productivity becomes a natural byproduct of consistent habits.

Consistency as the Foundation of Productivity

Productivity is built on a foundation of consistent, structured efforts. The establishment of productive habits provides the framework for sustained productivity. When tasks are approached with regularity and purpose, the efficiency and effectiveness of work increase, leading to heightened productivity.

The Ripple Effect: Productivity Beyond Habits

The impact of consistency extends beyond individual habits to create a ripple effect throughout various aspects of life. Consistent habits influence time management, goal achievement, and overall life satisfaction. The ripple effect of productivity reflects the holistic nature of the consistency-productivity relationship.

**Realizing Long-Term Goals through Consistency**

As individuals navigate their journey of completing initiatives, the role of consistency in realizing long-term goals becomes paramount. Long-term goals require sustained effort and a commitment to consistent actions over an extended period. Examining the strategies for maintaining consistency in the pursuit of long-term goals provides insights into the enduring power of this principle.

The Marathon Mentality

Long-term goals demand a marathon mentality—a steadfast commitment to the journey, despite challenges and setbacks. Consistency becomes the training regimen that prepares individuals for the endurance required in the pursuit of significant achievements. The marathon mentality embraces the journey as a series of consistent, purposeful strides.

Adaptability and Consistency

Consistency does not imply rigidity; it is a dynamic principle that embraces adaptability. Long-term goals may necessitate adjustments to strategies, habits, and timelines. The ability to adapt while maintaining a consistent commitment to the overarching goal ensures resilience in the face of changing circumstances.

Celebrating Milestones: Motivation for the Journey

The journey toward long-term goals is punctuated by milestones—markers of progress that signify achievements along the way. Celebrating milestones is not just a momentary indulgence; it is a crucial element of maintaining motivation and sustaining consistency. Milestone celebrations reinforce the connection between consistent efforts and tangible results.

**Overcoming Challenges in Consistency**

While the benefits of consistency are evident, individuals may encounter common challenges in maintaining habitual behaviors. Identifying and addressing these challenges contributes to the resilience required for long-term consistency.

Boredom and Monotony

Repetitive actions can lead to boredom and a sense of monotony, potentially derailing consistency. Overcoming boredom involves injecting variety into routines, setting periodic challenges, and cultivating a mindset that appreciates the nuances of consistency as a pathway to growth.

External Influences and Distractions

External influences, such as societal expectations or unexpected events, can disrupt consistent habits. Overcoming external influences requires a proactive approach to adaptability, clear prioritization of habits, and the cultivation of resilience to navigate unforeseen challenges without abandoning consistency.

Impatience and Instant Gratification

The desire for instant gratification can clash with the gradual nature of habit formation. Overcoming impatience involves cultivating a long-term perspective, acknowledging the incremental nature of progress, and appreciating the transformative power of consistent, sustained efforts over time.

Lack of Intrinsic Motivation

Consistency thrives on intrinsic motivation—the internal drive fueled by personal values and a genuine interest in the habits being established. Overcoming a lack of intrinsic motivation involves reconnecting with the deeper purpose behind habits, aligning them with personal values, and fostering a mindset that appreciates the intrinsic rewards of consistency.

**Case Studies in Consistency: Real-World Examples**

To illuminate the principles and strategies discussed, we turn to real-world case studies that exemplify the effective application of consistency in diverse contexts. These case studies provide insights into how individuals and organizations have harnessed the power of consistency to overcome challenges and achieve success.

Case Study 1: Professional Development Through Daily Learning

Sarah, a professional seeking continuous growth, committed to a habit of daily learning. She dedicated 30 minutes each day to reading articles, watching educational videos, or engaging in online courses. Despite a busy schedule, Sarah's consistency in daily learning led to a profound expansion of her knowledge and skill set over time. The habit of consistent learning became a cornerstone of her professional development, opening doors to new opportunities and advancements.

Case Study 2: Fitness Transformation Through Regular Exercise

John, on a quest for improved health and fitness, embraced a habit of regular exercise. Starting with short, consistent workouts three times a week, John gradually increased the intensity and duration over the months. His commitment to consistency in exercise not only resulted in physical transformations but also fostered mental resilience and discipline. The habit of regular exercise became a lifelong commitment that positively influenced various aspects of John's well-being.

Case Study 3: Entrepreneurial Success Through Daily Planning

Emma, an entrepreneur with a vision for business success, implemented a daily planning habit. Each morning, she dedicated 15 minutes to outline her priorities, set goals, and create a focused plan for the day. Emma's consistency in daily planning empowered her to stay organized, manage tasks efficiently, and navigate challenges with strategic foresight. The habit of consistent daily planning became a cornerstone of her entrepreneurial journey, contributing to the growth and sustainability of her ventures.

## The Lifelong Journey of Consistency

As we conclude our exploration into "The Power of Consistency: Establishing Productive Habits," it's crucial to recognize that consistency is not a destination but a lifelong journey. The principles and strategies discussed serve as a compass for navigating this journey with purpose, resilience, and a commitment to continuous improvement.

### Lifelong Learning and Adaptation

The journey of consistency is a continuous cycle of learning and adaptation. Each habit formed, each milestone achieved, contributes to personal and professional growth. The ability to adapt habits to evolving circumstances ensures that consistency remains a dynamic force that propels individuals toward their ever-evolving goals.

### Consistency Across Domains

The principles of consistency extend beyond professional initiatives; they encompass personal development, relationships, health, and well-being. The habits established in one domain influence others, creating a tapestry of consistent efforts that contribute to holistic growth and fulfillment.

### Mentorship and Passing on Wisdom

As individuals navigate their journey of consistency, the role of mentorship becomes invaluable. Passing on the wisdom gained through the experience of establishing and maintaining productive habits contributes to the collective growth of communities and societies.

## Conclusion

"The Power of Consistency: Establishing Productive Habits" is not just a chapter in a guidebook; it is a profound exploration into the principles that underpin meaningful achievements. By understanding the transformative power of consistency, embracing the strategies for habit formation, and applying intentional efforts, individuals can lay the groundwork for success that is enduring and fulfilling.

As we navigate the realms of consistency, may the insights shared in this chapter serve as a guide, empowering individuals to forge habits that propel them toward the completion of all initiatives. In the grand narrative of achieving success, consistency emerges as the steady rhythm that orchestrates the symphony of sustained effort, leading individuals to the pinnacle of their aspirations.

# 7. NAVIGATING CHALLENGES

## *Overcoming Obstacles Along the Way*

In the pursuit of any meaningful initiative, challenges and obstacles are inevitable companions on the journey. The path to success is seldom a smooth, unobstructed road; rather, it is a dynamic landscape marked by peaks and valleys, each presenting its unique set of challenges. In this chapter, we embark on a profound exploration of "Navigating Challenges: Overcoming Obstacles Along the Way," an indispensable guide within the comprehensive book, "Completing All Initiatives: A Guide to Success."

### The Inevitability of Challenges

Challenges are an integral part of the tapestry of success. Whether in personal or professional endeavors, the journey toward completing initiatives is fraught with uncertainties, setbacks, and unforeseen hurdles. Understanding and accepting the inevitability of challenges is the first step in developing the resilience required to navigate them effectively.

Dynamic Nature of Challenges

Challenges come in various forms and sizes, and their dynamic nature adds an element of unpredictability to any initiative. From external factors such as market shifts and economic fluctuations to internal challenges like self-doubt and resource constraints, the landscape of obstacles is multifaceted. Embracing the dynamic nature of challenges is essential for developing a proactive and adaptive mindset.

## The Relationship Between Challenges and Growth

Inherent within challenges is the potential for growth. Each obstacle, when approached with a constructive mindset, becomes an opportunity for learning, skill development, and personal evolution. Recognizing the symbiotic relationship between challenges and growth transforms setbacks into stepping stones on the path to success.

## The Psychological Landscape of Challenges

The impact of challenges extends beyond the tangible, external realm; it permeates the psychological landscape of individuals and organizations. Understanding the psychological dimensions of challenges is crucial for fostering resilience and maintaining a positive mindset in the face of adversity.

### The Psychology of Resilience

Resilience is the capacity to bounce back from setbacks and adapt to change. The psychology of resilience involves cultivating a mindset that views challenges as temporary hurdles rather than insurmountable barriers. Building resilience is a dynamic process that incorporates coping mechanisms, self-efficacy, and a belief in one's ability to navigate challenges.

### Emotional Responses to Challenges

Challenges elicit a range of emotions, from frustration and disappointment to anxiety and fear. Acknowledging and understanding these emotional responses is a vital aspect of navigating challenges effectively. Emotional intelligence, the ability to recognize and manage emotions, becomes a valuable skill in maintaining composure and making informed decisions during challenging times.

### The Role of Mindset in Overcoming Challenges

Mindset, the underlying framework of beliefs and attitudes, plays a pivotal role in how individuals approach challenges. A growth mindset, as opposed to a fixed mindset, fosters a belief in the capacity for learning and improvement. Cultivating a growth mindset enables individuals to view challenges as opportunities for development rather than insurmountable obstacles.

**Strategies for Navigating Challenges**

Effectively navigating challenges requires a strategic and proactive approach. The development of a toolkit of strategies empowers individuals and organizations to not only overcome obstacles but also thrive in the face of adversity.

Anticipate and Plan for Challenges

Proactivity is a cornerstone of effective challenge navigation. Anticipating potential challenges allows for strategic planning and risk mitigation. Conducting thorough scenario analysis, considering various contingencies, and formulating response plans create a foundation for navigating challenges with agility.

Cultivate Adaptive Leadership

In the face of challenges, leadership becomes a guiding force. Adaptive leadership involves the ability to navigate uncertainty, inspire resilience in teams, and make informed decisions amid ambiguity. Cultivating adaptive leadership skills empowers individuals to steer initiatives through turbulent waters and lead by example in embracing change.

Collaborate and Seek Support

The burden of challenges is lighter when shared. Collaboration and seeking support, whether from team members, mentors, or peers, create a network of resources and insights. Collective problem-solving harnesses diverse perspectives, fostering innovative solutions to challenges that may be insurmountable when faced in isolation.

Learn from Setbacks

Challenges often come hand in hand with setbacks. Viewing setbacks not as failures but as opportunities for learning is a fundamental mindset shift. Actively extracting lessons from setbacks informs future decision-making, enhances problem-solving skills, and contributes to continuous improvement.

Maintain Focus on Long-Term Goals

Amidst challenges, it's easy to lose sight of long-term goals. Maintaining a focus on the bigger picture provides a compass for decision-making. Evaluating the impact of challenges in the context of overarching goals helps prioritize actions and navigate challenges with a strategic perspective.

Embrace a Solution-Oriented Mindset

A solution-oriented mindset involves approaching challenges with a proactive focus on finding solutions rather than dwelling on problems. This mindset shift fosters a culture of innovation and resilience, where challenges are viewed as opportunities to implement positive change.

## Case Studies in Challenge Navigation

To illuminate the principles and strategies discussed, we turn to real-world case studies that exemplify effective challenge navigation in diverse contexts. These case studies provide insights into how individuals and organizations have successfully overcome obstacles and adversities on their path to completing initiatives.

Case Study 1: Tech Startup in a Competitive Market

Alex, the founder of a tech startup, faced the challenge of entering a highly competitive market. Recognizing the need for innovation, Alex embraced the challenge as an opportunity to differentiate the product. Through continuous market research, collaboration with industry experts, and a commitment to adaptability, the startup not only navigated the challenge but also emerged as a disruptive force in the market.

Case Study 2: Personal Development Amidst Career Transitions

Emily, a professional navigating career transitions, encountered challenges related to skill gaps and uncertainty. Instead of viewing these challenges as barriers, Emily embraced them as catalysts for personal development. Through targeted training, mentorship, and a proactive approach to skill acquisition, Emily not only overcame the challenges but also positioned herself for successful career transitions.

Case Study 3: Nonprofit Organization Adapting to Change

A nonprofit organization faced challenges stemming from changes in funding dynamics and shifting community needs. The leadership team recognized the importance of adaptability and engaged in strategic planning. By diversifying funding sources, collaborating with community stakeholders, and redefining program strategies, the organization not only navigated the challenges but also strengthened its impact.

## Resilience and Adaptability: Cornerstones of Challenge Navigation

Resilience and adaptability are the cornerstones of effective challenge navigation. As individuals and organizations encounter obstacles along the way, cultivating these qualities becomes paramount for not only overcoming challenges but thriving in the midst of uncertainty.

The Dynamics of Resilience

Resilience involves the capacity to bounce back from setbacks, learn from experiences, and maintain a positive outlook. It is a dynamic quality that can be cultivated through mindfulness, coping strategies, and a belief in one's ability to navigate challenges. The cultivation of resilience transforms challenges into opportunities for personal and professional growth.

Adaptability in the Face of Change

Adaptability is the ability to adjust to new conditions and navigate change effectively. In a rapidly evolving world, adaptability is a prized skill that enables individuals and organizations to thrive amidst uncertainty. Embracing change as a constant and approaching it with a flexible mindset positions individuals to navigate challenges with agility.

The Intersection of Resilience and Adaptability

The intersection of resilience and adaptability forms a powerful synergy. Resilience provides the emotional and cognitive fortitude to navigate setbacks, while adaptability equips individuals with the skills to pivot, innovate, and thrive in the face of change. Together, these qualities create a robust foundation for effective challenge navigation.

**Overcoming Common Challenges in Challenge Navigation**

While the strategies for navigating challenges are potent, individuals may encounter common challenges that require specific attention. Identifying and addressing these challenges contributes to the development of a resilient and adaptive approach to overcoming obstacles.

Decision Paralysis

In the face of complex challenges, individuals may experience decision paralysis—the inability to make informed decisions due to overwhelm. Overcoming decision paralysis involves breaking down challenges into manageable components, seeking input from trusted advisors, and utilizing decision-making frameworks to guide choices.

Fear of Failure

The fear of failure can be a significant barrier to effective challenge navigation. Overcoming this fear involves reframing failure as a natural part of the learning process, celebrating small successes along the way, and recognizing that setbacks are stepping stones to success. Cultivating a positive relationship with failure enhances resilience and fosters a growth mindset.

Resource Constraints

Limited resources, whether financial, human, or technological, can pose challenges to effective navigation. Overcoming resource constraints involves creative problem-solving, prioritization of essential tasks, and leveraging available resources strategically.

Resourcefulness becomes a key asset in navigating challenges with resilience.

Resistance to Change

Resistance to change, whether from individuals or within organizational cultures, can impede effective challenge navigation. Overcoming resistance involves effective communication, fostering a culture of adaptability, and highlighting the benefits of change. Engaging stakeholders in the change process creates a sense of ownership and collective commitment.

**Lessons from Challenges: Building a Foundation for Success**

Challenges, when navigated effectively, become invaluable lessons that contribute to the foundation of success. Reflecting on the lessons learned from challenges is a transformative process that informs future actions, strengthens resilience, and shapes the trajectory of initiatives.

Learning from Setbacks

Setbacks, though disheartening in the moment, offer profound learning opportunities. Actively reflecting on setbacks involves analyzing root causes, identifying areas for improvement, and incorporating lessons into future strategies. Learning from setbacks is a continuous, iterative process that fuels personal and professional growth.

Iterative Improvement: The Challenge Feedback Loop

Effective challenge navigation involves an iterative process of improvement. Each challenge navigated provides feedback that informs adjustments to strategies, enhances decision-making processes, and refines approaches. Embracing challenges as part of a continuous feedback loop creates a culture of adaptive improvement.

Building Confidence Through Challenge Navigation

Successfully navigating challenges enhances confidence. The experience of overcoming obstacles instills a belief in one's ability to handle adversity, fostering self-efficacy and a positive mindset.

Confidence becomes a valuable asset that propels individuals to take on increasingly complex initiatives with a sense of assurance.

**Case Study 4: Building a Global Brand in the Face of Economic Uncertainty**

Mark, an entrepreneur with a vision to build a global brand, faced the challenge of economic uncertainty. Instead of retreating in the face of external challenges, Mark embraced the opportunity to redefine the brand's value proposition, streamline operations, and explore new markets. Through strategic innovation, agile decision-making, and a commitment to customer-centricity, the brand not only weathered economic uncertainties but also emerged stronger and more resilient.

**Beyond Obstacles: Thriving in the Face of Challenges**

Thriving in the face of challenges goes beyond merely overcoming obstacles; it involves leveraging challenges as catalysts for innovation, growth, and transformation. As individuals and organizations navigate the complexities of completing initiatives, the ability to thrive amidst challenges becomes a hallmark of enduring success.

Innovation Through Adversity

Challenges stimulate innovation by necessitating creative problem-solving. Embracing challenges as opportunities to innovate involves seeking novel solutions, thinking outside conventional boundaries, and fostering a culture that values experimentation. Innovation through adversity positions individuals and organizations as industry leaders and pioneers.

Growth Mindset: Embracing Challenges as Opportunities

A growth mindset is the belief that abilities and intelligence can be developed through dedication and hard work. Embracing challenges as opportunities for growth aligns with a growth mindset. Cultivating this mindset involves viewing challenges not as threats but as avenues for stretching one's capabilities and expanding one's potential.

Transformational Leadership in the Face of Challenges

Leadership in the face of challenges extends beyond adaptive decision-making; it involves transformational leadership. Transformational leaders inspire teams to embrace challenges, foster a collective vision for success, and instill a sense of purpose amidst adversity. The transformative impact of leadership during challenges resonates far beyond the immediate obstacle.

**Conclusion: A Resilient Journey of Completion**

As we conclude our exploration into "Navigating Challenges: Overcoming Obstacles Along the Way," it's imperative to recognize that the journey of completing all initiatives is a resilient one. Challenges, far from being roadblocks, become milestones that mark the transformative journey toward success.

The Enduring Power of Resilience

Resilience is not a trait to be summoned sporadically; it is a dynamic force that permeates the entire journey. The enduring power of resilience lies in its ability to shape mindsets, fortify individuals and organizations, and propel them forward even in the face of formidable challenges.

Challenges as Catalysts for Achievement

Challenges, when navigated with resilience and adaptability, cease to be impediments; they become catalysts for achievement. Each challenge surmounted strengthens the foundation for subsequent successes, contributing to a narrative of growth, learning, and triumph.

The Uncharted Territories of Completion

Completing all initiatives is an exploration of uncharted territories—territories marked by challenges, discoveries, and triumphs. The resilience developed in navigating challenges becomes the compass that guides individuals through unexplored realms, transforming the journey into a resilient and fulfilling adventure.

As individuals and organizations embark on their journeys of completion, may the insights shared in this chapter serve as a compass, a source of inspiration, and a reminder that challenges, far from being deterrents, are integral elements of a transformative odyssey toward success. In the grand narrative of completing all initiatives, the ability to navigate challenges with resilience and adaptability emerges as the indomitable spirit that propels individuals and organizations to the summits of their aspirations.

# 8. EFFECTIVE TIME MANAGEMENT

## *Maximizing Your Productivity*

Success in any endeavor is often closely tied to how well one manages their time. Time is a finite resource, and its effective utilization can make the difference between completing all initiatives and falling short of your goals. In this chapter, we will delve into the art of effective time management, exploring strategies and techniques to help you maximize your productivity.

**The Importance of Time Management**

Time management is more than just a buzzword; it's a critical skill that can shape the trajectory of your personal and professional life. As the saying goes, "Time is money," and indeed, the way you use your time can determine your financial success, personal fulfillment, and overall well-being.

### 1. Setting Clear Goals

One of the fundamental principles of effective time management is setting clear, measurable goals. Without a clear destination, you risk meandering through tasks without a sense of purpose or direction. Whether your goals are short-term or long-term, they should be specific, achievable, relevant, and time-bound (SMART). This clarity provides a roadmap for your time management efforts.

### 2. Prioritizing Tasks

Not all tasks are created equal. Some have greater importance and urgency than others. The Eisenhower Matrix, a time management tool attributed to President Dwight D. Eisenhower, categorizes tasks into four quadrants: urgent and important, important but not urgent, urgent but not important, and neither urgent nor important. By prioritizing tasks based on this matrix, you can focus on what truly matters and avoid the trap of being busy but unproductive.

### 3. Effective Planning and Scheduling

A well-thought-out plan is the cornerstone of effective time management. This involves breaking down larger goals into smaller, manageable tasks and scheduling them realistically. Tools such as to-do lists, calendars, and project management apps can be invaluable in organizing your time. Allocate specific time slots for different activities, and be mindful of deadlines to ensure a proactive approach.

**Strategies for Effective Time Management**

Now that we've established the importance of time management, let's explore some practical strategies to help you make the most of your time.

### 1. The Pomodoro Technique

This time management method, developed by Francesco Cirillo, involves breaking your work into intervals, traditionally 25 minutes in length, separated by short breaks. These intervals are referred to as "Pomodoros." After completing four Pomodoros, take a longer break. This technique helps maintain focus and prevent burnout by providing regular, structured breaks.

### 2. Batching Similar Tasks

Batching involves grouping similar tasks together and tackling them during designated time blocks. This minimizes the cognitive load associated with switching between different types of activities and allows you to enter a state of flow. For example, answering emails, making phone calls, or working on specific project components can be batched to enhance efficiency.

### 3. The Two-Minute Rule

If a task takes less than two minutes to complete, do it immediately. This rule, popularized by productivity expert David Allen, prevents small tasks from accumulating and becoming overwhelming. By addressing quick tasks promptly, you maintain a sense of control over your workload.

### 4. Time Blocking

Time blocking involves scheduling specific blocks of time for different activities. Whether it's focused work, meetings, or personal time, allocating dedicated time slots enhances concentration and reduces multitasking. It also ensures that important but not urgent tasks receive the attention they deserve.

### 5. Learn to Say No

A crucial aspect of time management is knowing when to decline additional commitments. While it's tempting to take on more tasks to demonstrate productivity, overloading yourself can lead to burnout and decreased overall effectiveness. Learning to say no assertively, while respecting your existing commitments, is a skill that can significantly contribute to effective time management.

**Overcoming Time Management Challenges**

Despite our best intentions, challenges to effective time management inevitably arise. Recognizing and addressing these challenges is essential for maintaining a consistent and productive approach to your initiatives.

### 1. Procrastination

Procrastination is a common enemy of effective time management. Understanding the root causes of procrastination, such as fear of failure or lack of interest, is the first step in overcoming it. Break tasks into smaller, more manageable parts, set short deadlines, and leverage techniques like the Pomodoro Technique to counteract procrastination.

### 2. Interruptions and Distractions

In today's connected world, interruptions and distractions abound. Whether it's emails, social media, or the constant ping of notifications, these disruptions can derail your focus. Implement strategies to minimize interruptions, such as turning off non-essential notifications, designating specific times for email and social media, and creating a dedicated workspace.

### 3. Perfectionism

Striving for perfection can be a time-consuming endeavor. While high standards are commendable, perfectionism can lead to unnecessary delays. Recognize that perfection is often unattainable and that completing tasks to an acceptable standard within a reasonable timeframe is more beneficial than endlessly refining them.

## Leveraging Technology for Time Management

In the digital age, numerous tools and technologies are available to enhance time management. Leveraging these resources can provide a significant advantage in staying organized and productive.

### 1. Project Management Apps

Platforms like Asana, Trello, and Jira can streamline project workflows, enabling teams to collaborate effectively and stay on track. These tools offer features such as task assignment, progress tracking, and deadline reminders, enhancing overall project efficiency.

### 2. Time Tracking Software

Understanding how you spend your time is crucial for effective time management. Time tracking software, such as Toggl or RescueTime, can help you monitor your activities, identify time-wasting habits, and make informed decisions about how to allocate your time more effectively.

### 3. Calendar Apps

Calendar apps, like Google Calendar or Microsoft Outlook, are powerful tools for scheduling and organizing your time. Utilize features such as reminders, color-coding, and shared calendars to manage your appointments, deadlines, and commitments seamlessly.

## The Mind-Body Connection

Effective time management is not solely about optimizing schedules and tasks; it also involves taking care of your mental and physical well-being. A healthy mind and body contribute to sustained productivity and resilience in the face of challenges.

### 1. **Prioritize Self-Care**

Ensure that you allocate time for self-care activities, such as exercise, adequate sleep, and relaxation. A well-rested and healthy individual is better equipped to handle stress and maintain focus.

### 2. **Mindfulness and Meditation**

Incorporating mindfulness practices and meditation into your routine can improve your ability to concentrate and manage stress. These techniques enhance self-awareness and promote a calm, focused mindset, essential for effective time management.

## Continuous Improvement

Effective time management is a skill that can be honed and refined over time. Regularly assess your strategies and adjust them based on your evolving priorities and challenges. Solicit feedback from colleagues, mentors, or coaches to gain insights into areas for improvement.

## Conclusion

In the pursuit of completing all initiatives and achieving success, effective time management is non-negotiable. By setting clear goals, prioritizing tasks, and implementing proven strategies, you can maximize your productivity and navigate the complexities of modern life with confidence. Embrace the principles outlined in this chapter, leverage technology thoughtfully, and remember that time is a valuable resource that, once spent, cannot be reclaimed. Through mindful time management, you can not only complete all initiatives but also create a foundation for sustained success in all aspects of your life.

# 9. TEAMWORK AND COLLABORATION

## *Amplifying Your Success*

In the complex landscape of today's professional and personal endeavors, the ability to work effectively as part of a team is a key factor in completing all initiatives and achieving success. This chapter explores the importance of teamwork and collaboration, delving into strategies and principles that can amplify your success in various aspects of life.

**The Power of Teamwork**

### 1. Synergy: The Whole is Greater Than the Sum of its Parts

Teamwork is not just about individuals working side by side; it's about creating synergy, where the collective efforts of the team result in outcomes that exceed the contributions of individual members. This synergy taps into diverse perspectives, skills, and strengths, fostering creativity and innovation.

### 2. Division of Labor and Specialization

Teams allow for the division of labor, enabling individuals to focus on tasks that align with their strengths and expertise. This specialization leads to increased efficiency and higher-quality outcomes. By leveraging the unique skills of each team member, the overall productivity of the group is elevated.

### 3. Shared Responsibility and Accountability

In a well-functioning team, members share both responsibility and accountability. This shared ownership of goals and tasks fosters a sense of commitment and motivation. When individuals know that their contributions directly impact the success of the team, they are more likely to invest their time and energy wholeheartedly.

**Building Effective Teams**

Creating a successful team requires careful consideration of various factors, from team composition to communication strategies. Let's explore key elements that contribute to the formation and success of effective teams.

1. **Diverse Skill Sets and Perspectives**

A diverse team brings a range of skills, experiences, and perspectives to the table. This diversity not only enhances problem-solving by providing multiple viewpoints but also promotes a rich learning environment. Embrace differences in backgrounds, expertise, and personalities to create a well-rounded team.

2. **Clear Goals and Roles**

Establishing clear goals and defining individual roles are crucial for team success. Each member should understand the overall objectives of the team and how their contributions contribute to those goals. This clarity minimizes confusion, aligns efforts, and ensures everyone is working towards a common purpose.

3. **Effective Communication**

Open and effective communication is the lifeblood of any successful team. Foster an environment where team members feel comfortable expressing their ideas, concerns, and feedback. Utilize various communication channels, such as meetings, emails, and collaborative platforms, to ensure information flows seamlessly within the team.

4. **Trust and Mutual Respect**

Trust is the foundation of strong teams. Team members must trust one another's abilities, judgment, and commitment to the team's goals. Building trust requires time, consistent communication, and a willingness to be vulnerable. Mutual respect for each team member's contributions is equally vital.

## 5. Conflict Resolution Skills

Conflicts are inevitable in any team setting. What matters is how conflicts are managed. Equip your team with conflict resolution skills, encouraging open dialogue and addressing issues promptly. When conflicts are handled constructively, they can lead to enhanced understanding and stronger team cohesion.

## Collaboration in Professional Settings

## 1. Cross-Functional Collaboration

In today's interconnected world, collaboration often extends beyond individual teams to involve various departments and functions within an organization. Cross-functional collaboration breaks down silos, encourages knowledge sharing, and promotes a holistic approach to problem-solving.

## 2. Virtual Collaboration

The rise of remote work and global teams has highlighted the importance of effective virtual collaboration. Virtual collaboration tools, video conferencing, and cloud-based platforms enable teams to work seamlessly across geographical boundaries. Establishing clear communication norms and utilizing technology thoughtfully are essential for virtual collaboration success.

## 3. Innovation through Diversity

Diverse teams are not only more adaptable but also more innovative. Different perspectives foster creativity, challenging the status quo and driving the development of groundbreaking ideas. Embrace diversity not only for its intrinsic value but also as a catalyst for innovation in your initiatives.

## Overcoming Challenges in Teamwork

While teamwork is a powerful force, it is not without its challenges. Recognizing and addressing these challenges is crucial for maintaining a positive and productive team dynamic.

## 1. Communication Breakdowns

Effective communication is a double-edged sword; when it works well, it propels the team forward, but when it breaks down, it can lead to misunderstandings and conflicts. Encourage transparent communication, actively listen to team members, and address communication issues promptly to prevent them from escalating.

## 2. Lack of Accountability

In some teams, a lack of accountability can undermine the collective effort. Establish clear expectations for each team member, set measurable goals, and hold regular check-ins to review progress. When individuals are accountable for their contributions, the team is more likely to stay on track.

## 3. Resolving Conflicts

Conflict within a team is not inherently negative; in fact, it can lead to growth and improvement. However, when conflicts are left unresolved, they can fester and erode team morale. Provide tools and resources for conflict resolution, and create a culture where conflicts are viewed as opportunities for learning and improvement.

## Team Leadership and Empowerment

Effective team leadership is pivotal in harnessing the full potential of a team. A leader's role goes beyond simply delegating tasks; it involves inspiring, guiding, and empowering team members to reach their full potential.

## 1. Inspiration and Vision

A visionary leader inspires their team by providing a compelling vision and a sense of purpose. When team members understand how their work contributes to the larger picture, they are more motivated and engaged. Share your vision with passion and clarity to ignite enthusiasm within the team.

## 2. Empowerment and Delegation

Empowerment involves giving team members the autonomy to make decisions and take ownership of their work. Delegating tasks according to individual strengths and providing the necessary resources and support empowers team members to excel in their roles. This not only enhances productivity but also fosters a sense of pride and accomplishment.

## 3. Recognition and Feedback

Recognition is a powerful motivator. Acknowledge and celebrate the achievements of individual team members and the team as a whole. Constructive feedback, delivered with empathy and a focus on improvement, is equally important for continuous growth. Regularly check in with team members to provide guidance and support.

## The Role of Teamwork in Personal Initiatives

Teamwork is not confined to professional settings; it is equally relevant in personal initiatives and projects. Whether you're planning a family event, organizing a community project, or pursuing a personal goal, leveraging the principles of teamwork can amplify your success.

## 1. Family and Community Collaboration

In family and community settings, collaboration is essential for bringing people together and achieving shared objectives. Clearly define roles, communicate effectively, and tap into the strengths of each member to make collective initiatives more efficient and rewarding.

## 2. Mastermind Groups for Personal Development

Mastermind groups, popularized by Napoleon Hill in "Think and Grow Rich," bring individuals together to support each other's personal and professional development. These groups provide a platform for brainstorming, goal setting, and mutual accountability, creating a powerful synergy that propels each member towards success.

## Tools and Technologies for Collaboration

In the digital age, an array of tools and technologies can facilitate collaboration, whether in the workplace or for personal initiatives. Leveraging these tools thoughtfully can streamline communication, enhance productivity, and amplify the impact of teamwork.

## 1. Collaboration Platforms

Platforms like Slack, Microsoft Teams, and Trello facilitate real-time communication and collaboration. These tools offer features such as instant messaging, file sharing, and project management capabilities, creating a centralized hub for team activities.

## 2. Video Conferencing

Video conferencing tools, such as Zoom and Google Meet, bridge geographical gaps and enable face-to-face communication in virtual environments. Video meetings enhance the sense of connection and foster a more personal and collaborative atmosphere.

## 3. Cloud-Based Document Sharing

Collaborative document editing and sharing platforms, including Google Workspace and Microsoft 365, enable multiple users to work on documents simultaneously. This not only streamlines collaboration but also ensures that everyone has access to the latest version of shared documents.

## Conclusion

In the journey of completing all initiatives and achieving success, the power of teamwork and collaboration cannot be overstated. Whether in professional settings or personal pursuits, working effectively with others amplifies your capabilities and brings diverse strengths to the forefront. By fostering a culture of communication, trust, and accountability, and embracing the principles outlined in this chapter, you can harness the collective potential of a team to navigate challenges, drive innovation, and achieve success that transcends individual accomplishments. In the next chapter, we will explore resilience and adaptability as key qualities that complement effective teamwork, providing a comprehensive guide to success in the ever-evolving landscape of life and work.

# 10. CELEBRATING MILESTONES

## *Boosting Motivation Throughout*

In the pursuit of success and the completion of various initiatives, the journey is often marked by milestones—significant achievements that signify progress and accomplishment. This chapter explores the importance of celebrating milestones and how doing so can serve as a powerful motivator throughout the course of any endeavor.

**Recognizing the Significance of Milestones**

### 1. Building Momentum

Milestones are like stepping stones that pave the way to success. Each accomplishment, no matter how small, contributes to the momentum of a project or goal. Celebrating milestones not only acknowledges progress but also fuels the motivation to tackle the next set of challenges.

### 2. Tracking Progress

Milestones provide a tangible way to track progress. In the absence of milestones, the path forward may seem long and arduous. However, breaking down larger goals into smaller, achievable milestones creates a roadmap that makes the journey more manageable and progress more measurable.

### 3. Boosting Morale and Motivation

Achieving a milestone is a cause for celebration, and celebration, in turn, boosts morale and motivation. The sense of accomplishment, when acknowledged and shared, creates a positive and energizing environment. This positive reinforcement encourages individuals and teams to persevere, even in the face of challenges.

**Types of Milestones**

Milestones come in various forms, depending on the nature of the initiative. Recognizing and categorizing milestones can help in planning and structuring the journey toward success.

1. **Task Completion Milestones**

These milestones mark the completion of specific tasks or activities within a larger project. For example, in a product development initiative, a task completion milestone could be the successful testing and finalization of a prototype.

2. **Time-Based Milestones**

Time-based milestones are tied to specific timelines or deadlines. They ensure that progress is made within a predetermined timeframe. Meeting these milestones instills a sense of discipline and time management.

3. **Financial Milestones**

In business and financial initiatives, hitting certain financial targets or achieving specific revenue milestones is crucial. These milestones often serve as indicators of the project's financial health and viability.

4. **Learning and Skill Development Milestones**

Personal and professional development initiatives often involve learning and acquiring new skills. Milestones in these contexts may include completing a course, obtaining a certification, or mastering a specific skill set.

**The Art of Celebrating Milestones**

Celebrating milestones is more than just a momentary expression of joy; it's a deliberate and thoughtful process that reinforces the value of the achieved milestone. Here are some effective ways to celebrate milestones:

## 1. Recognition and Acknowledgment

Taking the time to recognize and acknowledge the efforts of individuals or teams involved in reaching a milestone is essential. This acknowledgment can be done publicly, through team meetings, emails, or even social media platforms, depending on the nature of the milestone.

## 2. In-Person or Virtual Celebrations

Organize celebrations to mark significant milestones. These can range from in-person events, such as team lunches or dinners, to virtual celebrations for remote teams. The key is to create an environment where individuals feel appreciated and celebrated.

## 3. Customized Rewards

Consider providing personalized or team-specific rewards for achieving milestones. This could include gift cards, additional time off, or even symbolic trophies or certificates. Tailoring the rewards to the preferences and values of the individuals involved adds a personal touch.

## 4. Reflective Activities

Encourage individuals or teams to reflect on the journey leading up to the milestone. This could involve sharing lessons learned, acknowledging challenges overcome, and expressing gratitude for the collective effort. Reflective activities provide a sense of closure and pave the way for the next phase of the initiative.

## 5. Communication of Impact

Clearly communicate the impact of the milestone on the overall initiative. Help individuals understand how their contributions have moved the needle and contributed to the broader success of the project or goal. This connection between individual efforts and overall impact enhances a sense of purpose and fulfillment.

## Milestones in Professional Settings

In the professional realm, celebrating milestones is not only about recognizing individual achievements but also about fostering a positive and collaborative work culture.

### 1. Project Completion Milestones

Projects in the workplace often have clear milestones tied to specific deliverables or phases. Celebrating the completion of a project or a major project phase is an opportunity to acknowledge the hard work and dedication of the entire team.

### 2. Sales and Revenue Milestones

For sales teams and businesses, achieving revenue targets or hitting sales milestones is a cause for celebration. Recognizing these achievements motivates the team to continue their efforts and may contribute to a competitive and success-driven culture.

### 3. Employee Service Milestones

Long-term commitment from employees is an asset to any organization. Acknowledging service milestones, such as work anniversaries, communicates appreciation for loyalty and dedication. This recognition can boost employee morale and contribute to a positive workplace culture.

### 4. Innovation and Product Development Milestones

Innovation is often a core focus in many industries. Milestones in product development, such as the launch of a new product or the successful implementation of innovative technologies, are opportunities to celebrate the creativity and hard work of the teams involved.

## Personal Milestones and Self-Celebration

While professional milestones are crucial, personal milestones are equally significant in the journey of self-improvement and fulfillment. Celebrating personal achievements contributes to a positive self-image and enhances overall well-being.

## 1. Fitness and Health Milestones

In personal wellness journeys, hitting fitness or health milestones, such as weight loss goals or achieving a personal best in a physical activity, is cause for celebration. Recognizing these achievements reinforces healthy habits and motivates continued effort.

## 2. Educational Milestones

Whether completing a degree, mastering a new language, or acquiring a new skill, educational milestones are opportunities for self-celebration. Acknowledge the time and effort invested in personal development and growth.

## 3. Personal Finance Milestones

Financial goals, such as saving a specific amount, paying off debt, or achieving a certain level of financial independence, are personal milestones that deserve recognition. Celebrating these achievements reinforces positive financial habits.

## 4. Relationship Milestones

In personal relationships, hitting milestones such as anniversaries or overcoming challenges together is a reason to celebrate. These celebrations contribute to the strength and resilience of relationships.

## The Psychological Impact of Milestone Celebrations

Beyond the immediate joy and satisfaction, celebrating milestones has a profound psychological impact on individuals and teams.

## 1. Positive Reinforcement

Positive reinforcement is a psychological concept that involves rewarding desired behavior to encourage its repetition. Celebrating milestones provides positive reinforcement for the efforts and behaviors that contributed to the achievement, reinforcing the motivation to continue those actions.

## 2. Sense of Progress and Achievement

Milestones create a tangible sense of progress and achievement. This sense of accomplishment is crucial for maintaining motivation and preventing burnout. It serves as a reminder of what is possible through sustained effort and dedication.

### 3. Enhanced Well-Being

Recognition and celebration contribute to enhanced well-being. Positive emotions associated with achievements, such as pride and happiness, have a ripple effect on mental and emotional health. This, in turn, contributes to a positive outlook and increased resilience in the face of challenges.

### 4. Cultivation of a Growth Mindset

Celebrating milestones aligns with the principles of a growth mindset, a concept developed by psychologist Carol Dweck. A growth mindset is characterized by a belief in the ability to grow and develop through effort and learning. Celebrating milestones reinforces the idea that progress is achievable through dedication and continuous improvement.

## Cultivating a Milestone-Centric Culture

To truly leverage the power of milestone celebrations, it's essential to cultivate a culture that values and prioritizes these moments of achievement.

### 1. Leadership Example

Leaders play a crucial role in shaping organizational culture. When leaders actively participate in and endorse milestone celebrations, it sends a powerful message about the importance of acknowledging and appreciating achievements.

### 2. Integrated into Performance Management

Integrate milestone celebrations into performance management processes. This could involve recognizing achievements during performance reviews, tying financial incentives to the accomplishment of certain milestones, or incorporating celebration events into regular team meetings.

### 3. Fostering Peer Recognition

Encourage peer-to-peer recognition as part of the celebration culture. This creates a supportive and collaborative atmosphere where individuals appreciate and celebrate each other's successes. Peer recognition enhances team cohesion and camaraderie.

### 4. Documentation and Reflection

Documenting milestones and the associated celebrations contributes to a sense of history and achievement within an organization or team. Additionally, periodic reflections on past milestones can inspire and motivate individuals to reach new heights.

## Overcoming Challenges in Milestone Celebrations

While celebrating milestones is essential, challenges may arise in the process. Addressing these challenges ensures that celebrations remain meaningful and contribute to sustained motivation.

### 1. Balancing Individual and Team Recognition

Striking the right balance between individual and team recognition can be challenging. While it's crucial to acknowledge individual contributions, it's equally important to celebrate the collective effort. Clearly communicate the criteria for recognition to avoid potential misunderstandings.

### 2. Avoiding Complacency

While celebrating achievements, there's a risk of complacency setting in. It's essential to balance celebration with a forward-looking mindset. Use milestone celebrations as opportunities to set new goals and challenges, ensuring continued growth and progress.

### 3. Inclusive Celebrations

In diverse teams or organizations, it's essential to ensure that milestone celebrations are inclusive and considerate of various cultural and individual preferences. Create a flexible framework that allows for personalized and inclusive celebrations.

### 4. Balancing Long-Term and Short-Term Milestones

In complex projects or initiatives, there may be both short-term and long-term milestones. Balancing the celebration of immediate wins with the recognition of progress toward long-term goals is crucial. This approach maintains motivation over the entire duration of the initiative.

**Milestones and Adaptability**

In the dynamic landscape of life and work, adaptability is a key quality. Milestone celebrations can play a role in fostering adaptability by providing moments of reflection and learning.

1. **Adapting Goals**

Milestone celebrations provide an opportunity to assess whether goals need to be adapted or refined. This adaptability ensures that initiatives remain aligned with evolving priorities and circumstances.

2. **Learning from Challenges**

Not all milestones are reached without facing challenges. Milestone celebrations should include a reflective component that considers the lessons learned from obstacles encountered. This learning contributes to a more informed and adaptable approach moving forward.

3. **Celebrating Iterative Progress**

In iterative processes or projects, where progress involves cycles of improvement, celebrating milestones becomes an ongoing and adaptive practice. Recognizing incremental improvements fosters a culture of continuous learning and refinement.

**Technology and Milestone Tracking**

In the digital age, technology plays a crucial role in milestone tracking and celebration. Leveraging technology can enhance the efficiency and effectiveness of the celebration process.

1. **Project Management Tools**

Project management tools, such as Trello, Asana, or Jira, provide features for setting, tracking, and visualizing project milestones.

These tools facilitate transparent communication and collaboration among team members.

## 2. Social Media and Internal Platforms

Utilize social media or internal communication platforms for publicizing and celebrating milestones. This not only amplifies the recognition but also fosters a sense of pride and accomplishment among team members.

## 3. Gamification

Incorporate gamification elements into milestone tracking. Gamification adds a competitive and fun dimension to achieving milestones, making the process more engaging. Leaderboards, badges, and other gamified elements can enhance the celebration experience.

## The Role of Milestones in Resilience

Resilience is the ability to bounce back from setbacks and navigate challenges effectively. Milestone celebrations contribute to the development of resilience in several ways.

## 1. Positive Reinforcement in the Face of Challenges

During challenging times, milestone celebrations serve as positive reinforcement. They remind individuals and teams of their capabilities and past successes, instilling confidence and resilience to overcome current challenges.

## 2. Cultivating a Positive Mindset

The regular practice of celebrating milestones contributes to cultivating a positive mindset. A positive mindset is a foundational element of resilience, enabling individuals to approach challenges with optimism and determination.

## 3. Fostering a Supportive Environment

Milestone celebrations create a supportive and encouraging environment. In times of adversity, this sense of support from colleagues and leaders can be a crucial factor in building resilience.

Knowing that achievements are recognized and celebrated fosters a sense of belonging and camaraderie.

## Conclusion

In the journey of completing all initiatives and achieving success, celebrating milestones emerges as a pivotal practice. Whether in professional or personal endeavors, the deliberate acknowledgment of achievements contributes to motivation, resilience, and a positive mindset. As we navigate the ever-evolving landscape of life and work, the consistent practice of celebrating milestones becomes not only a marker of progress but also a catalyst for continuous growth and success. In the next chapter, we will explore the qualities of adaptability and resilience as essential components of a comprehensive guide to success.

# 11. ADAPTING TO CHANGE

## *Flexibility in the Pursuit of Goals*

In the intricate dance of life and ambition, change is the only constant. Navigating through the ever-evolving landscape of personal and professional endeavors requires a key quality: adaptability. This chapter explores the significance of adapting to change and the flexibility required in the pursuit of goals, providing insights and strategies to thrive in an environment that is inherently dynamic.

**Embracing the Nature of Change**

### 1. The Inevitability of Change

Change is an inherent part of the human experience. From shifting personal circumstances to dynamic professional landscapes, the ability to adapt is a fundamental skill in the pursuit of success. Recognizing the inevitability of change sets the stage for a proactive and resilient mindset.

### 2. The Paradox of Stability and Change

While stability provides a sense of security, it is essential to acknowledge that stability itself is subject to change. Embracing this paradox allows individuals to develop a mindset that is both rooted in the present and open to the possibilities that change brings.

### 3. Opportunities Amidst Challenges

Change is often accompanied by challenges, but within those challenges lie opportunities for growth and innovation. The ability to discern and capitalize on these opportunities distinguishes those who merely survive change from those who thrive in it.

## The Importance of Adaptability in Goal Achievement

### 1. Flexibility as a Strategic Advantage

In the pursuit of goals, rigid adherence to a predetermined plan may lead to stagnation. Flexibility, on the other hand, is a strategic advantage. Being open to adapting plans and strategies allows for responsiveness to changing circumstances and a more nuanced approach to goal achievement.

### 2. Resilience in the Face of Setbacks

Adaptability and resilience go hand in hand. When faced with setbacks or unexpected challenges, individuals who possess a high degree of adaptability bounce back more effectively. Resilience is not about avoiding challenges but about navigating them with a flexible and forward-looking perspective.

### 3. Continuous Learning and Improvement

Adaptability fosters a culture of continuous learning and improvement. Those who are open to change are more likely to seek out new information, embrace diverse perspectives, and refine their approaches. This commitment to growth positions individuals for long-term success.

## Strategies for Developing Adaptability

### 1. Cultivating a Growth Mindset

A growth mindset, as proposed by psychologist Carol Dweck, is the belief that abilities and intelligence can be developed through dedication and hard work. Cultivating a growth mindset is foundational to adaptability. It involves viewing challenges as opportunities to learn and improve, rather than as insurmountable obstacles.

### 2. Embracing Change as a Learning Experience

Rather than resisting change, approach it as a learning experience. Analyze the factors driving the change, identify potential opportunities for growth, and extract lessons that can inform future decisions. This proactive approach transforms change from a source of anxiety to a catalyst for development.

### 3. Building a Supportive Network

Surrounding oneself with a diverse and supportive network is crucial for adaptability. A network provides varying perspectives, insights, and advice that can be invaluable in navigating change. Seeking input from others fosters a collaborative approach to problem-solving and decision-making.

### 4. Developing Emotional Intelligence

Emotional intelligence, including self-awareness, self-regulation, empathy, and interpersonal skills, plays a significant role in adaptability. Being attuned to one's emotions and those of others enables individuals to navigate change with resilience and maintain effective relationships amid uncertainty.

### 5. Setting Milestones Instead of Rigid Plans

While planning is essential, rigid plans can become obstacles in the face of change. Instead of setting rigid plans, establish milestones. Milestones provide flexibility in adjusting the approach while still maintaining a sense of progress toward overarching goals.

## Adapting to Change in Professional Settings

### 1. Agile Project Management

Agile project management is a methodology that emphasizes flexibility and responsiveness to change. In Agile, projects are broken down into small, iterative cycles, allowing for continuous reassessment and adaptation. This approach is particularly effective in dynamic and rapidly changing environments.

### 2. Open Communication Channels

In professional settings, open communication channels are crucial for adaptability. Encourage transparent communication within teams, ensuring that information flows freely. This transparency enables quick identification of emerging challenges and facilitates collaborative problem-solving.

### 3. Encouraging a Culture of Innovation

A culture of innovation thrives on adaptability. Encourage team members to explore new ideas, experiment with different approaches, and embrace calculated risks. An innovative culture fosters an environment where change is viewed as an opportunity rather than a disruption.

### 4. Professional Development Opportunities

Providing professional development opportunities for employees fosters adaptability. Continuous learning and skill development not only enhance individual capabilities but also contribute to a workforce that is agile and capable of meeting evolving industry demands.

### Adapting to Change in Personal Pursuits

### 1. Adjusting Personal Goals

In personal pursuits, the ability to adjust goals in response to changing circumstances is vital. While long-term aspirations provide direction, the journey may involve detours and unexpected turns. Being open to adjusting personal goals allows for a more realistic and sustainable approach to success.

### 2. Balancing Flexibility with Commitment

Flexibility should not be misconstrued as a lack of commitment. Rather, it involves adapting the approach while staying committed to the overarching goal. Striking the right balance between flexibility and commitment is essential for enduring success.

### 3. Mindful Decision-Making

Mindful decision-making involves considering the potential long-term consequences of choices and being aware of the need for adaptability. Before making decisions, assess how they align with overarching goals and whether they allow for the flexibility needed to navigate change.

### 4. **Cultivating a Supportive Personal Network**

In personal pursuits, a supportive network is equally important. Surround yourself with individuals who understand your goals, offer encouragement, and provide constructive feedback. A supportive network can be a source of inspiration and resilience during times of change.

### **Resilience as a Companion to Adaptability**

### 1. **The Interplay of Resilience and Adaptability**

Resilience and adaptability are interconnected qualities that complement each other. While adaptability involves adjusting to change, resilience is the capacity to bounce back from setbacks. Together, they form a robust foundation for navigating the complexities of life and work.

### 2. **Learning from Setbacks**

Resilience involves learning from setbacks rather than being defeated by them. When faced with challenges, individuals with high resilience leverage the experience as an opportunity for growth, adapting their strategies for future success.

### 3. **Coping Mechanisms in Times of Stress**

Developing healthy coping mechanisms is an integral aspect of resilience. Whether through mindfulness practices, physical exercise, or other stress-relief activities, individuals can cultivate a reservoir of resilience that sustains them during challenging periods of change.

### 4. **Building Mental and Emotional Toughness**

Mental and emotional toughness are key components of resilience. This involves developing the capacity to withstand adversity without losing sight of one's goals. Resilience enables individuals to navigate change with a sense of purpose and determination.

**Technology and Adaptability**

In the digital age, technology plays a significant role in facilitating adaptability. Leveraging technology tools and platforms can enhance the ability to respond to change effectively.

1. **Remote Collaboration Tools**

Remote collaboration tools, such as video conferencing and project management platforms, enable teams to stay connected and work seamlessly, regardless of geographical locations. These tools enhance the adaptability of teams in the face of evolving work structures.

2. **Data Analytics for Informed Decision-Making**

Data analytics provides valuable insights that inform decision-making. In both professional and personal pursuits, the ability to analyze data allows individuals to adapt strategies based on real-time information, enhancing the likelihood of success.

3. **Online Learning Platforms**

Online learning platforms offer a flexible and accessible means of acquiring new skills. Embracing continuous learning through online courses and certifications enhances adaptability by ensuring individuals remain current in their fields.

**Overcoming Challenges in Adaptability**

1. **Fear of the Unknown**

The fear of the unknown can be a significant barrier to adaptability. Overcoming this fear involves reframing change as an opportunity for growth and learning. Developing a curious and open mindset toward the unknown fosters a proactive approach to change.

2. **Resistance to Change**

Resistance to change is a common challenge in both personal and professional settings. Addressing this resistance requires effective communication, transparency about the reasons for change, and involving individuals in the decision-making process when possible.

### 3. Overcoming Cognitive Biases

Cognitive biases, such as the status quo bias or the anchoring effect, can hinder adaptability. Overcoming these biases involves self-awareness and deliberate efforts to consider alternative perspectives and approaches.

### 4. Balancing Stability and Adaptability

Finding the right balance between stability and adaptability is an ongoing challenge. While adaptability is crucial, stability provides a foundation for growth. Striking the right balance involves assessing the context and determining when to pivot and when to stay the course.

## Adapting to Change as a Lifelong Skill

### 1. A Continuous Journey

Adapting to change is not a one-time event but a continuous journey. Lifelong learning, curiosity, and a commitment to personal and professional growth are essential components of this journey. Embracing change as a constant allows for a more proactive and empowered approach to life.

### 2. The Evolution of Goals

As individuals evolve, so do their goals. Adapting to change involves recognizing when goals need to be reassessed and realigned with current priorities. This evolution ensures that goals remain relevant and meaningful over the course of a lifetime.

### 3. Legacy and Impact

Adapting to change extends beyond personal success to the impact one leaves on the world. Those who navigate change with resilience and adaptability contribute not only to their own success but also to the broader legacy of positive change and progress.

## Conclusion

In the pursuit of completing all initiatives and achieving success, adaptability emerges as a cornerstone quality. The ability to navigate change with resilience and flexibility is not only a survival skill but a catalyst for growth and innovation. As we explore the dynamic interplay of adaptability, resilience, and the other qualities outlined in this guide, we unlock the potential to thrive in the face of complexity and uncertainty. In the final chapter, we will bring together the key principles discussed throughout the book, providing a comprehensive guide to success in the ever-changing landscape of life and work.

# 12. MINDFULNESS IN ACTION

## *Enhancing Concentration and Clarity*

In the fast-paced and dynamic world we navigate, the ability to stay focused and maintain clarity amidst myriad distractions is a valuable skill. This chapter delves into the transformative power of mindfulness in action, exploring how it enhances concentration, cultivates clarity, and contributes to success in completing various initiatives.

### Understanding Mindfulness

### 1. The Essence of Mindfulness

At its core, mindfulness is the practice of being fully present and engaged in the current moment. It involves cultivating awareness without judgment, allowing individuals to observe thoughts and emotions with clarity. Mindfulness is not merely a meditative practice; it is a way of being that permeates every aspect of life.

### 2. The Mind-Body Connection

Mindfulness emphasizes the connection between the mind and the body. By paying attention to bodily sensations, breath, and the present environment, individuals can anchor themselves in the moment. This heightened awareness fosters a deeper understanding of the interplay between mental and physical states.

### 3. Present-Moment Focus

The present moment is where life unfolds, decisions are made, and actions are taken. Mindfulness encourages a shift from dwelling on the past or anticipating the future to a focused awareness of the current moment. This shift is foundational to enhancing concentration and clarity.

## Mindfulness and Concentration

### 1. Overcoming Distractions

In a world teeming with distractions, maintaining concentration can be challenging. Mindfulness provides a powerful antidote by training individuals to bring their attention back to the present whenever distractions arise. This heightened awareness allows for a more sustained and focused engagement with tasks.

### 2. Enhancing Attention Span

The ability to sustain attention on a single task is crucial for productivity. Mindfulness practices, such as meditation and mindful breathing, have been shown to enhance attention span. Regular practice strengthens the "muscle" of attention, enabling individuals to stay focused for more extended periods.

### 3. Cultivating Deep Work

Deep work, a term coined by productivity expert Cal Newport, refers to the ability to focus without distraction on a cognitively demanding task. Mindfulness facilitates the cultivation of deep work by training individuals to resist the pull of constant connectivity and immerse themselves fully in the task at hand.

## Mindfulness and Clarity

### 1. Quieting the Mental Chatter

The mind is often filled with a continuous stream of thoughts, worries, and distractions. Mindfulness acts as a gentle guide to quieting this mental chatter. By observing thoughts without judgment, individuals create space for clarity to emerge, allowing for more informed decision-making.

### 2. Emotional Regulation and Clarity

Mindfulness involves acknowledging and accepting emotions without being overwhelmed by them. This emotional regulation contributes to mental clarity. When individuals are not clouded by intense emotional reactions, they can approach situations with a calm and rational perspective.

## 3. Seeing Things as They Are

Mindfulness encourages seeing things as they truly are, unfiltered by preconceptions or biases. This clear perception enables individuals to assess situations objectively, make accurate assessments, and respond effectively. Clarity of perception is a cornerstone of wise decision-making.

## Mindfulness Practices for Concentration and Clarity

### 1. Mindful Breathing

Mindful breathing involves directing full attention to the breath, observing its natural rhythm. This practice anchors individuals in the present moment and serves as a readily accessible tool to bring the mind back to focus when distractions arise.

### 2. Body Scan Meditation

The body scan meditation involves systematically bringing attention to different parts of the body, promoting a heightened awareness of bodily sensations. This practice not only enhances mindfulness but also contributes to physical relaxation, reducing overall stress levels.

### 3. Mindful Walking

Mindful walking is a practice of walking with deliberate awareness of each step and the sensations associated with movement. It can be practiced indoors or outdoors, offering a simple yet effective way to integrate mindfulness into daily activities.

### 4. Focused Attention Meditation

Focused attention meditation involves concentrating on a specific object, thought, or sensation. This practice hones the skill of sustained attention, fostering a capacity for deep concentration.

### 5. Mindful Eating

Mindful eating involves paying full attention to the sensory experience of eating, including the taste, texture, and smell of food. This practice not only enhances the enjoyment of meals but also cultivates mindfulness in daily activities.

## Mindfulness in Professional Settings

### 1. Enhancing Decision-Making

In professional settings, where decisions carry significant weight, mindfulness enhances decision-making. By reducing the impact of cognitive biases and emotional reactions, individuals can approach decisions with a clear and discerning mind.

### 2. Effective Communication

Mindfulness contributes to effective communication by fostering active listening and presence. In meetings and collaborative settings, individuals who practice mindfulness are better equipped to absorb information, respond thoughtfully, and contribute meaningfully to discussions.

### 3. Stress Reduction and Resilience

Work environments can be inherently stressful. Mindfulness practices act as stress-reduction tools, helping individuals manage work-related pressures more effectively. The cultivation of resilience through mindfulness ensures that individuals bounce back from challenges with greater ease.

### 4. Cultivating a Mindful Workplace Culture

Leaders play a pivotal role in cultivating a mindful workplace culture. When leaders prioritize and model mindfulness practices, it sets a tone for the entire organization. Mindful workplaces are characterized by increased focus, improved decision-making, and a more positive work environment.

## Mindfulness in Personal Pursuits

### 1. Balancing Work and Personal Life

Mindfulness facilitates the balance between work and personal life. By being fully present in each domain, individuals can maximize their engagement and satisfaction in both professional and personal pursuits. This balance contributes to overall well-being.

## 2. Enhancing Creativity

Creativity flourishes in a mind that is open, receptive, and free from excessive mental clutter. Mindfulness practices foster a creative mindset by creating the conditions for novel ideas to emerge and encouraging a non-judgmental approach to the creative process.

## 3. Mindfulness for Stress Management

Personal pursuits often come with their own set of stressors. Mindfulness serves as a personal stress-management tool, allowing individuals to navigate challenges with a composed and clear-minded approach. The ability to manage personal stress contributes to long-term success.

## The Neuroscience of Mindfulness

## 1. Neuroplasticity and Mindfulness

Neuroplasticity, the brain's ability to reorganize and adapt, is influenced by mindfulness practices. Studies have shown that regular mindfulness practice can lead to structural changes in the brain, particularly in areas associated with attention, emotion regulation, and self-awareness.

## 2. The Default Mode Network

The default mode network (DMN) is a network of brain regions associated with mind-wandering and self-referential thoughts. Mindfulness practices have been found to modulate the activity of the DMN, reducing excessive rumination and promoting present-moment awareness.

## 3. Increased Grey Matter Density

Research suggests that mindfulness practitioners may exhibit increased grey matter density in regions of the brain associated with learning, memory, and emotional regulation. These structural changes align with the observed cognitive and emotional benefits of mindfulness.

**Mindfulness in the Digital Age**

**1. Digital Detox and Mindfulness**

In an era of constant connectivity, a digital detox is a mindful practice in itself. Taking intentional breaks from digital devices allows individuals to reclaim their attention and cultivate mindfulness in the face of technological distractions.

**2. Mindful Technology Use**

Mindful technology use involves approaching digital tools with awareness and intention. This includes setting boundaries on screen time, being present in virtual interactions, and using technology as a tool for productivity rather than succumbing to mindless scrolling.

**3. Mindfulness Apps and Platforms**

Technology also offers mindfulness resources, including apps and platforms that guide individuals through meditation and mindfulness practices. These tools make mindfulness accessible and convenient, particularly for those navigating busy schedules.

**Overcoming Challenges in Practicing Mindfulness**

**1. The Myth of Multitasking**

Multitasking, often perceived as a productivity booster, is a challenge to mindfulness. The brain is not designed for true multitasking, and attempting to juggle multiple tasks simultaneously can hinder concentration and clarity. Mindfulness encourages a focused and single-tasking approach.

**2. Impatience and Frustration**

Impatience and frustration can arise when individuals expect immediate results from mindfulness practices. It's essential to approach mindfulness with a sense of openness and patience, recognizing that the benefits may unfold gradually over time.

### 3. Inconsistency in Practice

Consistency is key to reaping the full benefits of mindfulness. Inconsistency in practice may limit its impact. Establishing a regular mindfulness routine, even if brief, contributes to the cultivation of lasting habits.

### 4. Cultural and Organizational Barriers

In some cultures and organizations, the concept of mindfulness may face resistance or skepticism. Addressing cultural and organizational barriers involves education, communication, and demonstrating the practical benefits of mindfulness in enhancing concentration and clarity.

## Mindfulness as a Lifelong Companion

### 1. Integrating Mindfulness into Daily Life

Mindfulness is not confined to meditation sessions; it is a way of life. Integrating mindfulness into daily activities, such as eating, walking, or even washing dishes, ensures that it becomes a seamless and integrated part of one's routine.

### 2. Mindfulness as a Lifelong Journey

The journey of mindfulness is ongoing and evolves over a lifetime. As individuals grow and face new challenges, mindfulness adapts to meet the changing needs of the present moment. It is a lifelong companion on the path to success.

### 3. Legacy of Mindfulness

As individuals complete various initiatives and achieve success, the legacy of mindfulness extends beyond personal accomplishments. The practice of mindfulness ripples outward, influencing relationships, workplaces, and communities, fostering a culture of presence, focus, and clarity.

## Conclusion

In the pursuit of completing all initiatives and achieving success, mindfulness in action emerges as a transformative practice. By enhancing concentration, cultivating clarity, and fostering a present-moment awareness, mindfulness becomes a guiding force in navigating the complexities of life and work. As we conclude this comprehensive guide to success, we reflect on the interconnected qualities of adaptability, resilience, mindfulness, and others, recognizing their collective power in shaping a life of purpose, fulfilment, and achievement.

# 13. THE ART OF SAYING 'NO'

## *Prioritizing Your Initiatives*

In the intricate tapestry of professional and personal life, the ability to say 'no' is a strategic skill that empowers individuals to focus on what truly matters. This chapter explores the art of saying 'no,' delving into the nuances of effective prioritization and providing insights on how mastering this skill is pivotal to completing all initiatives and achieving success.

**The Power of 'No'**

### 1. Saying 'No' as a Positive Choice

Contrary to common perception, saying 'no' is not a rejection but a strategic choice. It is an assertion of one's priorities and a recognition of personal limits. Embracing the power of 'no' allows individuals to direct their energy toward initiatives that align with their overarching goals.

### 2. The Myth of Endless Yeses

The pressure to say 'yes' to every request can be overwhelming. The myth of endless yeses stems from a desire to please others and avoid conflict. However, this approach often leads to overcommitment, burnout, and a dilution of focus on key priorities.

### 3. Setting Boundaries for Success

Saying 'no' is about setting boundaries that safeguard one's time, energy, and resources. These boundaries are not obstacles but essential guardrails that guide individuals toward their most meaningful and impactful initiatives. Boundaries create the space for success to flourish.

**The Psychology of Saying 'No'**

### 1. **Overcoming the Fear of Disappointment**

The fear of disappointing others is a common barrier to saying 'no.' However, recognizing that saying 'no' is not a personal rejection but a strategic decision can alleviate this fear. Understanding that clear communication about priorities is respectful and appreciated fosters a healthier mindset.

### 2. **The Empowerment of Prioritization**

Saying 'no' empowers individuals to be the architects of their own success. It is a declaration of autonomy and a commitment to prioritizing initiatives that align with personal and professional goals. Prioritization is a key element in the journey of completing all initiatives.

### 3. **Protecting Mental and Emotional Well-Being**

Overcommitment can take a toll on mental and emotional well-being. Saying 'no' is a form of self-care that protects against stress, burnout, and a sense of overwhelm. It allows individuals to invest their energy where it matters most.

**The Strategic Art of Saying 'No'**

### 1. **Aligning with Core Values**

The strategic art of saying 'no' begins with a clear understanding of core values. When requests or opportunities align with these values, saying 'yes' becomes a strategic choice. Conversely, saying 'no' to divergent initiatives ensures alignment with overarching principles.

### 2. **Assessing Impact and Contribution**

Every initiative carries a level of impact and contribution. Assessing the potential impact of saying 'yes' or 'no' helps individuals prioritize initiatives that align with their goals. It involves considering the long-term value of each commitment.

### 3. Maintaining a Focus on Key Goals

Saying 'no' is an act of focus. It involves maintaining clarity on key goals and strategic priorities. By avoiding the distraction of peripheral initiatives, individuals can direct their efforts toward what truly matters for success.

### 4. Creating a Strategic Roadmap

A strategic roadmap serves as a guide for decision-making. It involves mapping out key initiatives, deadlines, and milestones, allowing individuals to see the bigger picture. This visual representation facilitates informed choices about where to invest time and resources.

### The Impact on Professional Life

### 1. Enhancing Professional Reputation

Saying 'no' strategically enhances professional reputation. It communicates a clear sense of purpose and reliability. Colleagues and collaborators appreciate working with individuals who are intentional about their commitments and deliver consistently.

### 2. Avoiding Burnout and Overwhelm

Overcommitment in a professional setting can lead to burnout and overwhelm. Saying 'no' to non-essential tasks or projects ensures that energy is directed toward high-impact initiatives, contributing to sustained success and well-being.

### 3. Fostering Effective Team Collaboration

Effective team collaboration relies on clear communication and shared understanding of priorities. Saying 'no' when necessary fosters a culture of open communication and respect. Team members can trust that when someone says 'yes,' it is a commitment that will be honored.

### 4. Building a Strategic Network

Building a strategic professional network involves making intentional choices about where to invest time and effort. Saying 'no' to peripheral networking opportunities allows individuals to focus on building meaningful connections that contribute to their professional goals.

## The Impact on Personal Life

### 1. Balancing Personal and Professional Commitments

Balancing personal and professional commitments requires a thoughtful approach to saying 'no.' It involves recognizing personal priorities and making choices that align with overall well-being. Striking this balance is crucial for sustained success and fulfillment.

### 2. Protecting Quality Time with Loved Ones

Quality time with loved ones is a precious commodity. Saying 'no' to non-essential commitments ensures that individuals can prioritize and protect these relationships. The art of saying 'no' extends beyond the professional realm to create space for personal connections.

### 3. Investing in Personal Growth

Saying 'no' strategically creates the space for personal growth initiatives. Whether it's pursuing further education, engaging in hobbies, or dedicating time to self-reflection, the ability to say 'no' empowers individuals to invest in their ongoing development.

### 4. Creating a Fulfilling Personal Life

A fulfilling personal life is built on intentional choices. Saying 'no' to commitments that do not align with personal values contributes to a life that is rich in meaning and purpose. It allows individuals to craft a narrative of success that extends beyond professional achievements.

## Practical Strategies for Saying 'No'

### 1. The Polite Decline

Crafting a polite decline involves expressing gratitude for the opportunity while clearly and respectfully declining. This approach acknowledges the request and communicates the decision with courtesy.

### 2. Setting Clear Boundaries

Setting clear boundaries involves communicating expectations regarding time, availability, and capacity. By proactively establishing boundaries, individuals reduce the likelihood of being overwhelmed by excessive commitments.

### 3. Using the 'Yes, If' Technique

The 'Yes, If' technique involves expressing openness to a request with certain conditions. This allows individuals to negotiate terms that align with their priorities while maintaining a collaborative approach.

### 4. Referencing Prior Commitments

Referencing prior commitments is a tactful way to decline new requests. By explaining existing obligations and commitments, individuals convey a sense of responsibility and reliability.

### 5. The Empathetic 'No'

The empathetic 'no' involves expressing understanding and empathy for the request while firmly declining. This approach acknowledges the needs of others while prioritizing one's own commitments.

## Overcoming Challenges in Saying 'No'

### 1. Fear of Missing Out (FOMO)

The fear of missing out is a common challenge in saying 'no.' Overcoming FOMO involves recognizing that every 'yes' comes with an implicit 'no' to other opportunities. By focusing on the chosen path, individuals can mitigate the anxiety of missing out.

### 2. Guilt and Obligation

Feelings of guilt and obligation often accompany the decision to say 'no.' It's essential to reframe these emotions by recognizing that saying 'no' is an act of self-care and a commitment to honoring existing obligations.

### 3. Effective Communication

Effective communication is crucial in overcoming challenges associated with saying 'no.' Clearly expressing reasons for the decision, whether they involve existing commitments, capacity limitations, or strategic priorities, fosters understanding.

## 4. Cultivating Assertiveness

Cultivating assertiveness is a key component of mastering the art of saying 'no.' Assertiveness involves communicating one's needs and boundaries with confidence and clarity. This skill empowers individuals to navigate requests assertively and respectfully.

## Saying 'No' as a Lifelong Skill

## 1. Evolving Priorities Over a Lifetime

Priorities evolve over a lifetime, necessitating an ongoing mastery of the art of saying 'no.' As individuals grow, develop, and face new challenges, the ability to prioritize remains essential for sustained success and fulfillment.

## 2. Navigating Career Transitions

Career transitions often come with a flurry of new opportunities and requests. Saying 'no' strategically during career transitions ensures that individuals remain focused on initiatives that align with their evolving professional goals.

## 3. Creating a Legacy of Purposeful Choices

The art of saying 'no' contributes to a legacy of purposeful choices. As individuals reflect on their journey, the decisions to say 'yes' and 'no' define the narrative of success they leave behind—a narrative rooted in intention, focus, and fulfillment.

## Conclusion

In the culmination of this guide to success, the art of saying 'no' emerges as a potent force for prioritizing initiatives and achieving meaningful accomplishments. By recognizing the power of strategic choices, individuals navigate the complexities of professional and personal life with intention, focus, and resilience. As we conclude this comprehensive exploration, we celebrate the interconnected qualities of adaptability, resilience, mindfulness, and the art of saying 'no,' recognizing their collective impact on a life of purpose, completion, and success.

# 14. LEARNING FROM SETBACKS

## *Turning Failures into Stepping Stones*

In the pursuit of success and the completion of various initiatives, setbacks and failures are inevitable companions on the journey. However, the true measure of an individual's resilience and determination lies in their ability to learn from setbacks, transforming them from stumbling blocks into stepping stones. This chapter explores the profound concept of learning from setbacks, delving into the psychology behind resilience, practical strategies for overcoming failures, and the enduring wisdom that emerges from the process.

**Understanding Setbacks as Inevitable**

### 1. The Inevitability of Setbacks

Setbacks are an inherent part of any ambitious endeavor. Whether in personal or professional pursuits, unexpected challenges, obstacles, and failures are bound to arise. Recognizing the inevitability of setbacks is the first step towards cultivating a mindset that views them not as roadblocks but as opportunities for growth.

### 2. The Myth of Smooth Success Paths

The myth of smooth success paths often leads individuals to underestimate the challenges they may face. Real success is not a linear journey but a series of peaks and valleys. Understanding this reality prepares individuals to navigate setbacks with resilience and determination.

### 3. Embracing a Growth Mindset

A growth mindset, as proposed by psychologist Carol Dweck, involves seeing challenges as opportunities for learning and growth. Embracing a growth mindset in the face of setbacks allows individuals to view failures as temporary setbacks rather than permanent defeats.

## The Psychology of Resilience

### 1. Resilience as a Psychological Asset

Resilience is the psychological asset that empowers individuals to bounce back from setbacks with newfound strength. It involves developing the capacity to endure adversity, adapt to change, and maintain a sense of purpose in the face of challenges.

### 2. The Role of Self-Efficacy

Self-efficacy, a concept introduced by psychologist Albert Bandura, is the belief in one's ability to succeed in specific situations or accomplish a task. High self-efficacy contributes to resilience by fostering confidence in one's ability to overcome setbacks through effort and determination.

### 3. Cultivating Emotional Intelligence

Emotional intelligence, encompassing self-awareness, self-regulation, empathy, and interpersonal skills, plays a crucial role in resilience. Understanding and managing one's emotions in the aftermath of setbacks enables individuals to navigate challenges with greater clarity and composure.

## Strategies for Learning from Setbacks

### 1. Reflection and Self-Awareness

Reflection is a powerful tool for learning from setbacks. Taking the time to reflect on the circumstances, decisions, and actions leading to the setback provides valuable insights. Self-awareness allows individuals to identify patterns, strengths, and areas for improvement.

## 2. Seeking Constructive Feedback

Constructive feedback is a valuable resource for growth. Seeking feedback from mentors, colleagues, or trusted friends provides an external perspective that can shed light on blind spots and offer guidance on how to address challenges more effectively.

## 3. Analyzing Root Causes

Understanding the root causes of setbacks goes beyond surface-level analysis. It involves delving into the underlying factors, whether they be external circumstances, internal dynamics, or unforeseen variables. Identifying root causes is key to implementing lasting solutions.

## 4. Applying the Growth Mindset

Applying the growth mindset involves reframing setbacks as opportunities for learning and development. Instead of viewing failures as reflections of personal inadequacy, individuals with a growth mindset see them as natural occurrences that contribute to their ongoing journey of improvement.

## Wisdom Gained from Setbacks

## 1. Adaptability and Flexibility

Setbacks often necessitate adaptability and flexibility. Learning from challenges requires the ability to reassess plans, pivot when necessary, and adjust strategies to align with evolving circumstances. The wisdom gained from setbacks includes a heightened capacity for navigating change.

## 2. Resilience and Perseverance

Resilience and perseverance are enduring qualities cultivated through the process of overcoming setbacks. The wisdom gained involves recognizing that setbacks are not roadblocks but temporary detours on the path to success. Perseverance ensures that individuals press on despite the challenges.

### 3. Improved Decision-Making

Setbacks provide a wealth of information that contributes to improved decision-making. Analyzing past decisions and their outcomes allows individuals to refine their judgment, consider alternative approaches, and make more informed choices in the future.

### 4. Enhanced Problem-Solving Skills

Facing setbacks fosters the development of enhanced problem-solving skills. The wisdom gained involves a honed ability to identify challenges, formulate creative solutions, and navigate complexities with a strategic mindset. Each setback becomes a lesson in effective problem-solving.

## Overcoming Setbacks in Professional Settings

### 1. Building a Supportive Team Culture

In professional settings, a supportive team culture is crucial for overcoming setbacks. Cultivating an environment where team members feel comfortable sharing failures and seeking help fosters collaboration and collective problem-solving.

### 2. Encouraging Innovation and Experimentation

A culture that encourages innovation and experimentation is more resilient in the face of setbacks. When individuals feel empowered to try new approaches and take calculated risks, setbacks become opportunities for discovery and improvement.

### 3. Leadership in Times of Setbacks

Leaders play a pivotal role in guiding teams through setbacks. Effective leadership involves providing support, acknowledging challenges, and inspiring confidence in the team's ability to overcome obstacles. Leaders who model resilience contribute to a culture of success.

### 4. Continuous Learning and Professional Development

Setbacks are integral to the learning process in professional development. Encouraging continuous learning and professional development ensures that individuals and teams stay current, adapt to industry changes, and build the skills necessary to overcome setbacks.

## Overcoming Setbacks in Personal Pursuits

### 1. Maintaining a Growth-Oriented Mindset

In personal pursuits, maintaining a growth-oriented mindset is essential for overcoming setbacks. This mindset involves embracing challenges as opportunities for personal growth and reframing setbacks as stepping stones toward self-improvement.

### 2. Cultivating Personal Resilience

Cultivating personal resilience involves developing coping mechanisms and strategies to navigate setbacks. Whether through mindfulness practices, social support, or self-care activities, individuals can enhance their capacity to endure and bounce back from challenges.

### 3. Aligning Actions with Personal Values

Aligning actions with personal values is a guiding principle for overcoming setbacks in personal pursuits. When setbacks occur, individuals who are anchored in their values can reassess their path, make adjustments, and continue moving forward with authenticity and purpose.

### 4. Building a Network of Support

Building a network of support is crucial for navigating setbacks in personal life. Friends, family, mentors, and peers can provide encouragement, perspective, and practical advice. This support network becomes a source of strength during challenging times.

## The Role of Setbacks in the Journey of Success

### 1. Redefined Notions of Success

Setbacks have the power to redefine notions of success. Through the process of overcoming challenges, individuals often discover that success is not a destination but a dynamic and evolving journey. The wisdom gained reshapes the understanding of what it truly means to succeed.

## 2. Fostering Humility and Empathy

Setbacks cultivate humility by revealing the inherent vulnerability in the pursuit of goals. This humility, in turn, fosters empathy for others facing challenges. The shared experience of setbacks creates a sense of connection and understanding among individuals on the path to success.

## 3. Contributing to a Resilient Mindset

A resilient mindset, forged through overcoming setbacks, is a lasting legacy on the journey to success. The ability to face adversity with courage, learn from failures, and emerge stronger contributes not only to personal growth but also to the collective resilience of communities and organizations.

## Turning Setbacks into Stepping Stones

## 1. Embracing the Growth Process

Setbacks are integral to the growth process. Embracing this process involves acknowledging that setbacks are not failures but opportunities for refinement, improvement, and the acquisition of wisdom. Each setback becomes a stepping stone toward personal and professional development.

## 2. Celebrating Progress, Not Perfection

Progress, not perfection, is the true measure of success. Celebrating the small victories, lessons learned, and personal growth that accompany setbacks reinforces a positive mindset. The journey is a series of steps, and setbacks are inherent in the path of progress.

## 3. Maintaining a Forward-Focused Perspective

A forward-focused perspective involves directing attention to the path ahead rather than dwelling on past setbacks. While learning from failures is essential, maintaining a focus on future goals and initiatives ensures that setbacks serve as foundations for continued success.

## Conclusion

In the concluding chapter of "Completing All Initiatives: A Guide to Success," the profound significance of learning from setbacks emerges as a central theme. Setbacks, when viewed through the lens of resilience, wisdom, and growth, cease to be barriers and transform into invaluable stepping stones on the journey to success. As we reflect on the interconnected qualities explored throughout this comprehensive guide—adaptability, resilience, mindfulness, the art of saying 'no,' and the transformative power of setbacks—we recognize that completion is not just about reaching the destination but embracing the entirety of the journey with courage, fortitude, and an unwavering commitment to growth.

# 15. CULMINATING SUCCESS

## *Reflections on a Journey of Completion*

In the intricate tapestry of life, the pursuit of success is not merely about reaching endpoints but encompasses the entirety of the journey. This chapter serves as a reflective culmination, inviting individuals to explore the essence of success, the transformative power of completion, and the wisdom gained along the way. As we navigate through the diverse landscapes of adaptability, resilience, mindfulness, the art of saying 'no,' and the profound lessons learned from setbacks, we arrive at the summit of achievement—a place where success is not just a destination but a state of being.

### The Essence of Success

### 1. Success Beyond External Metrics

While external metrics such as achievements, accolades, and tangible outcomes are markers of success, the essence of success extends beyond these parameters. True success encompasses personal growth, fulfillment, and the alignment of actions with one's values and aspirations.

### 2. The Journey as the Destination

The journey itself is a destination—a culmination of experiences, challenges, and triumphs that shape an individual's character and perspective. Recognizing the significance of the journey reframes success as an ongoing process rather than a singular achievement.

### 3. Embracing a Holistic Definition

Embracing a holistic definition of success involves considering various dimensions of life, including professional accomplishments, personal relationships, well-being, and contributions to the community. A comprehensive view of success ensures a balanced and fulfilling life.

## The Transformative Power of Completion

### 1. Completion as a Catalyst for Growth

Each completed initiative serves as a catalyst for personal and professional growth. The act of completion involves overcoming challenges, honing skills, and acquiring wisdom. It is a testament to resilience, adaptability, and the ability to navigate complexities.

### 2. Reflections on Achieved Goals

Reflection on achieved goals provides an opportunity to celebrate milestones, acknowledge hard work, and express gratitude for the journey. It involves savoring the sense of accomplishment and recognizing the impact of dedication and perseverance.

### 3. Creating a Legacy of Success

The legacy of success extends beyond individual achievements to the positive influence one leaves on others and the broader community. Completion becomes a way of contributing to a legacy characterized by integrity, purpose, and a commitment to making a difference.

## Lessons from Adaptability

### 1. Navigating Change with Grace

Adaptability is a cornerstone of success, enabling individuals to navigate change with grace and resilience. Reflecting on the lessons of adaptability involves recognizing the capacity to pivot, adjust, and thrive amidst evolving circumstances.

### 2. Embracing the Unpredictable

Life is inherently unpredictable, and adaptability involves embracing this unpredictability with openness and resourcefulness. The ability to thrive in dynamic environments becomes a valuable asset in the journey of completion.

### 3. Iterative Learning and Growth

Adaptability fosters iterative learning and growth. Reflecting on the iterative nature of personal and professional development involves recognizing that setbacks, challenges, and adaptations contribute to an ongoing process of refinement.

## Insights from Resilience

### 1. Bouncing Back from Setbacks

Resilience is the capacity to bounce back from setbacks stronger than before. Reflecting on resilience involves acknowledging the ability to endure challenges, learn from failures, and emerge with increased fortitude.

### 2. Building Inner Strength

The journey of completion builds inner strength through the challenges faced and overcome. Reflecting on the development of resilience involves recognizing the resilience gained as a profound inner resource.

### 3. Navigating Ambiguity and Uncertainty

Resilience is particularly crucial in navigating ambiguity and uncertainty. Reflecting on the role of resilience in the face of the unknown involves recognizing the power to confront uncertainties with courage and confidence.

## Wisdom from Mindfulness

### 1. Present-Moment Awareness

Mindfulness emphasizes present-moment awareness as a key to success. Reflecting on mindfulness involves recognizing the transformative power of being fully engaged in the current moment and the impact of focused attention on initiatives.

### 2. Cultivating Clarity and Concentration

Mindfulness contributes to clarity and concentration. Reflecting on the cultivation of these qualities involves acknowledging the role of mindfulness practices in enhancing decision-making, problem-solving, and sustained focus.

### 3. Integrating Mindfulness into Daily Life

Mindfulness is not confined to specific practices but extends into daily life. Reflecting on the integration of mindfulness involves recognizing moments of awareness, presence, and intentionality in various aspects of life.

## The Art of Saying 'No' and Prioritization

### 1. Strategic Decision-Making

The art of saying 'no' is a strategic skill in prioritizing initiatives. Reflecting on this skill involves recognizing the power of intentional choices, setting boundaries, and aligning actions with overarching goals.

### 2. Creating Space for Priorities

Saying 'no' creates space for essential priorities. Reflecting on the art of saying 'no' involves acknowledging the freedom it brings to direct energy toward initiatives that truly matter and contribute to long-term success.

### 3. Balancing Commitments

Prioritization, facilitated by the art of saying 'no,' is essential for balancing commitments. Reflecting on the ability to balance personal and professional pursuits involves recognizing the importance of intentional decision-making.

## Gleanings from Learning from Setbacks

### 1. Embracing Failure as a Teacher

Learning from setbacks involves embracing failure as a teacher rather than a deterrent. Reflecting on setbacks involves recognizing the transformative power of challenges in providing valuable lessons and insights.

## 2. Building Resilience through Adversity

Setbacks contribute to the building of resilience through adversity. Reflecting on resilience involves acknowledging the strength gained from overcoming setbacks and the ability to navigate future challenges with greater confidence.

## 3. Fostering a Growth Mindset

Learning from setbacks fosters a growth mindset. Reflecting on this mindset involves recognizing that setbacks are not indicative of personal limitations but opportunities for growth, refinement, and continuous improvement.

## Integrating Insights for Culminating Success

## 1. The Interconnectedness of Qualities

Reflecting on the journey of completion involves recognizing the interconnectedness of qualities explored throughout this guide. Adaptability, resilience, mindfulness, the art of saying 'no,' and the lessons from setbacks converge to shape a holistic and successful life.

## 2. Navigating the Complexity of Life

Completion is about navigating the complexity of life with intention, purpose, and adaptability. Reflecting on the interconnected qualities involves acknowledging their collective influence in shaping a journey marked by meaningful accomplishments.

## 3. Celebrating the Journey

As individuals reflect on the journey of completion, there is a celebration of the myriad experiences, the lessons learned, and the growth achieved. Reflecting on the journey involves celebrating not just the destinations but the process of becoming.

## Beyond Culmination - A Continuum of Success

## 1. Success as a Dynamic Continuum

Culminating success is not the end but a point along a dynamic continuum. Reflecting on success involves recognizing that the journey of completion extends into the future, presenting new opportunities for growth, learning, and contribution.

2. **The Ongoing Pursuit of Excellence**

Reflecting on completion involves embracing the ongoing pursuit of excellence. Success is not a static state but a commitment to continuous improvement, innovation, and a dedication to making a positive impact on the world.

3. **Legacy and Impact**

Culminating success is an opportunity to reflect on the legacy and impact one leaves. Reflecting on the broader implications of success involves considering how personal achievements contribute to the well-being of others and the betterment of society.

**Conclusion**

In the closing reflections of "Completing All Initiatives: A Guide to Success," the journey of completion emerges as a profound tapestry woven with threads of adaptability, resilience, mindfulness, the art of saying 'no,' and the transformative power of setbacks. As individuals navigate the intricate landscapes of personal and professional development, the essence of success is revealed not only in achievements but in the depth of growth, the wisdom gained, and the enduring commitment to continuous improvement. Culminating success is not a destination but a vantage point from which individuals embark on the next phase of their dynamic and purposeful journey—a journey marked by the ongoing pursuit of excellence, a legacy of impact, and the unwavering commitment to completing all initiatives with courage, intention, and resilience.

Milton Keynes UK
Ingram Content Group UK Ltd.
UKHW050740271123
433341UK00017B/1064